THE NOWHERE BOYS

To the late John T. Henderson, MA, OBE, JP,
who suggested and encouraged this research

The Nowhere Boys

A Comparative Study of Open and Closed Residential Placement

CAIRINE PETRIE

North East List D Psychological Service, Scotland

SAXON HOUSE

Published by

Saxon House, Teakfield Limited,
Westmead, Farnborough, Hampshire, England

Printed in Great Britain by
Biddles Ltd., Guildford, Surrey

British Library Cataloguing in Publication Data

Petrie, Cairine

The nowhere boys.
1. Juvenile detention homes–Scotland–Case studies
I. Title
365'.42 HV9147

ISBN 0 566 00302 3

Contents

Tables

Figures

Foreword

During the last two decades in the United Kingdom, we have increasingly locked up children who are difficult or delinquent. This study explores the uses and consequences of custody for young people.

Cairine Petrie compares a number of boys held in a unit of maximum security with a similar number of delinquents resident in an open training school. The book also provides interesting insights into the workings of the Scottish List D schools which, unlike institutions for young offenders in England and Wales, still remain the responsibility of the central authorities. South of the border since 1969, persistent delinquents have been sheltered in community homes and are in the care of the local authorities. Those who cling to the myth that effective reformatory schools have been swept away by permissive legislation will gain little comfort from this book.

The rapid failure of young offenders from several schools is clearly demonstrated. Cairine Petrie reminds us of the findings of many other research investigations; that the removal of young offenders from the community for a residential reformatory experience is expensive and ineffective. She finds that three-quarters of the boys returned to the outside world are reconvicted, the majority rapidly return to residential settings and few of those experiencing maximum security remain free after release for longer than two months. The study also indicates the vulnerability to prosecution of children from deprived families and, although not necessarily the most delinquent, once in our criminal processing system, these young offenders seem to remain in it.

Disturbing questions are also raised about the operation of maximum security for young people in Scotland. Ostensibly set up to take those boys which other schools could not hold, secure units are intended to contain the hard core of recalcitrant offenders who thwart the caring efforts of open institutions. If such 'rotten apples' exist, they do not seem to end up in the secure units. Cairine Petrie shows that incarcerated boys do not differ appreciably from those offenders sheltered in open conditions. Boys who end up in secure units are distinguished by their frequency of transfer between residential institutions. Indeed, these Scottish findings replicate recent studies of maximum security in England and Wales which demonstrate that clients for security have been long in care and are casualties created by the child care system itself.

This research also provides disturbing evidence on the number of mentally handicapped boys sheltered in List D schools, the problems that young offenders face in returning to their day schools and the acute employment problems of others. But the residential institutions are not held responsible for this sad situation, they are seen as struggling to change in a few brief months the self-perceptions and survival strategies that young offenders have taken a lifetime to fashion. The book should provide a short, sharp shock to those who advocate facile answers to the complex problem of persistent juvenile crime.

Spencer Millham
Dartington Social Research Unit
July 1979

Acknowledgements

The author is grateful to the managers of the school studied for their permission to undertake the research, to the headmasters and the staff for their help and advice, and mostly to the boys themselves.

Dr C.K. Mackay helped and advised on the statistics, and D.A.F. Conochie gave valuable help in discussing problems which arose in writing the work.

Ian Stephen, principal clinical psychologist in Polmont Borstal Institution, searched his records for names of boys in our study who had passed through Polmont for assessment, and thus provided valuable material for Chapter 8. The writer's warmest thanks are due to him for this kindness.

Gratitude is also due to the directors of social work in the regions and to their social workers who provided the follow-up information on the boys after release.

Social Work Service Group made available the necessary resources.

My warmest thanks are due to Mrs Howie, Mrs Muir and Miss McCabe, who patiently and expertly did the typing. Mrs Howie recorded the data from my psychological reports during the course of her secretarial work with me and this has formed the data basis of the study.

The Nowhere Man

He's a real Nowhere man,
Sitting in his Nowhere land,
Making all his Nowhere plans,
For Nobody.

Doesn't have a point of view,
Knows not where he's going to,
Isn't he a bit like you
And me?

Nowhere man, please listen,
You don't know what you're missing.
Nowhere man the world is at
Your command.
He's as blind as he can be,
Just sees what he wants to see,
Nowhere man can you see me
At all?

Nowhere man don't worry, take your time,
Don't hurry.
Leave it all till somebody else lends you
A hand.
Making all his Nowhere plans for Nobody.

Words and music by Lennon/McCartney

'On the temple gate he (i.e. Daedalus) pictured the murder of Androgeos the son of the king of Crete, and, lower down the Athenians obeying the ghastly command to surrender seven of their stalwart sons as annual reparation; and there was the urn from which the lots had just been drawn. The island on which Cnossos stands (i.e. Crete) rising high above the sea balanced the scene on the other leaf of the gate . . .'

Virgil: THE AENEID,
translated by W.F. Jackson Knight
(Penguin Classics, 1956) p.147

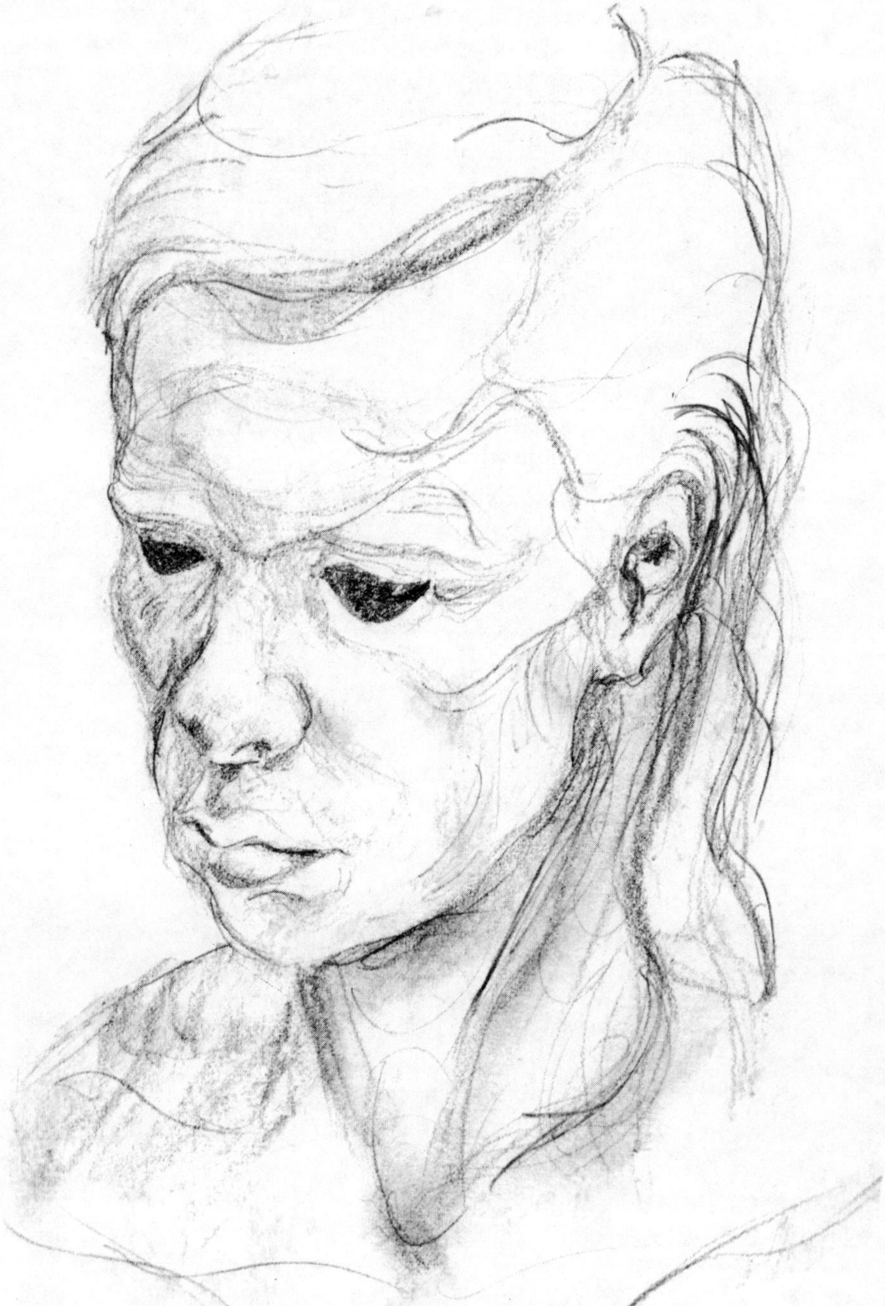

Duncan MacLean

1 Introduction

The study is a comparison of two groups of boys in Forest School, 100 consecutive cases from the 'Open' school and 100 consecutive cases from the high security unit, the Carpenter Wing. The school is for delinquent boys undergoing compulsory residential care.

The Forest School dates from 1856 and was instituted as a reformatory for teenage boys in an attempt to keep them out of adult prisons. The school is situated in a sparsely populated area, three miles from the sea, and lying below the Cairngorm mountains. It is remote from the cities from which its boys are drawn, and is surrounded by farming land and forest. Originally the school had its own farm which the boys worked. The aim of its originators was philanthropic, in common with that of the many contemporary Victorian institutions for deprived and delinquent children. Boys were retained originally for long periods, sometimes up to eight years, often proceeding thereafter to the Armed Services. Home contacts, should they have existed, would inevitably have been lost, for most boys came from the large cities geographically remote and leave was not allowed. Contemporaneously with the Forest School until the 1930s boys were also held in a prison hulk, the *Mars*, anchored in a neighbouring Scottish firth.

In addition to farming, trades were taught: building, gardening, carpentry, forestry, and shoemaking. These trades supplied two functions, teaching for the boys and the maintenance of the building and grounds. To some minimal extent therefore the school was self-maintaining in food from the farm and in upkeep from the boys' own labour. Some instruction in the three 'Rs' took place.

In 1939 the school was moved into a new building, built to house 90–100 boys. In common with the thinking of that time it was military in design, with 'block' dormitories, dining and washing and recreation facilities. The regime also was military in concept.

In 1962, in response to the demands from other approved schools in Scotland, and the report on the Carlton School riots in England, a 'secure unit' for 20 boys was built as a 'wing' to the school. This was the first secure unit in Britain and was designed to hold 'difficult, dangerous and disruptive' boys with whom other schools could not cope. Its role was to support other schools which found such boys beyond their control by removing them and retaining them in secure conditions.

Purpose of the research

The purpose of the research is to enquire if differences exist between the two groups of boys and to develop understanding of their circumstances.

The present situation

Since the Social Work (Scotland) Act 1968 schools have changed somewhat in character. Formerly they were named 'approved schools' but are now 'List D'—a name merely denoting the administrative category into which they fall. Rehabilitation, treatment, and the needs of the child are the new 'naming' words. Social workers are now on the staff, some trained—if only on one year courses—and education is more seriously considered. In Scotland at present there are 26 such List D schools with a population of some 1,200 to 1,500 children. Six of these schools are for girls. The Carpenter Wing is one of the secure units for Scottish boys, and further units are now on stream.

The boys in the study

The boys in the open school are fourteen and a half years and over on entry while the boys in the closed wing can be accepted from twelve and a half years of age (see Table 7.1). The boys in the latter are therefore heterogeneous in age, some young, but some may have passed their seventeenth birthday before release. The open school boys are more homogeneous in years. Boys in either group are rarely accepted at sixteen years or over since most older boys in trouble are dealt with by the courts, unless they are still under supervision from the Hearings due to previous events in their history.

Sources of committal

The Hearings

The Hearings are peculiarly Scottish and were instituted by the Social Work (Scotland) Act 1968. Their purpose is to identify and try to devise arrangements to meet the needs of children under sixteen who have offended and have accepted the charges made against them, or who may be in need of care for whatever reason. The emphasis is on care and the needs of the child, not 'punishment'. The Hearing is intended to be a panel of 'concerned and insightful adults, helping the child and his family' (*Children's Hearings,* 1970).

The Social Work (Scotland) Act 1968 in Section 32(2) lays down the conditions whereby a child may be called before a Hearing as being in need of 'compulsory measures of care' as follows:

(a) he is beyond the control of his parents; or
(b) through lack of parental care he is falling into bad associations or is exposed to moral danger; or
(c) that lack of care as aforesaid is likely to cause him unnecessary suffering or seriously impair his health and development; or
(d) any of the offences mentioned in Schedule 1 of the Children and Young Persons (Scotland) Act 1937 has been committed in respect of him or in respect of a child who is a member of the same household; or
(e) the child being a female is a member of the same household as a female in respect of whom an offence which constitutes the crime of incest has been committed by a member of that household; or
(f) he has failed to attend school without reasonable excuse; or
(g) he has committed an offence; or
(h) he is a child whose case has been referred to a Children's Hearing in pursuance of Part V of this Act (i.e. to do with absconding and transfer).

(3) For the purposes of this part of the Act 'care' includes protection, control, guidance and treatment.

It should be noted that 'committal of an offence' ranks low in Section 32(2) at (g), the care of the child having priority.

If the child is deemed by the Hearing to require compulsory residential placement a review can be sought by the parents or the child himself through the social worker within three months, or six months, but must occur within a year. Usually children spend ten to eleven months in residential placement, but the review by the panel may extend the length of time if this is considered desirable in the interests of the child.

Children placed by the Hearings in List D schools are paid for jointly by their own regions and the Social Work Services Group, and a contribution is also required from parents who have financial means. (For further study the reader is referred to the HMSO works listed in the bibliography.)

A decade of experience in the working of the panels has brought out strengths and weaknesses. (Martin and Murray 1976, Morris and McIzaac 1978.) A further work by Martin and Murray on the Hearings system is now in progress, financed by the USA State Department due to the interest expressed there in the Scottish system. Nevertheless, except for this American interest and also that of Quebec, which has borrowed largely from the Kilbrandon thinking in its latest reform of Juvenile Law (Leblanc 1979), Hearings are little known outside Scotland. The literature which exists is largely directed to Scottish readers as professional material for Hearing members and social workers. An international audience might well expand this major social advance in the care of children, now well established and accepted by the Scottish public.

The Sheriff Court

The Sheriff Court is involved if children deny the complaints brought against them but if these complaints are upheld then the child is referred back to the Hearings for disposal.

The Sheriff Court also considers cases of children under sixteen who commit offences along with an adult; for Road Traffic Act offences and for offences adjudged to be serious. The Sheriff, however, for a child under sixteen, or between sixteen and eighteen, if he has been on supervision after a previous appearance before a hearing, must refer to the Hearings for advice on disposal. The Sheriff, nevertheless, having taken cognizance of the hearing's advice is bound under the Criminal Procedure (Scotland) Act 1975, if the child is found guilty, by Section 413 or Section 206(1) or 206(2). Section 413 proceedings are for summary prosecution and Sections 206(1 and 2) for prosecution under indictment and for offences considered serious.

Section 413 of the Act states:

> Where a child is charged before the Sheriff with an offence he pleads guilt to, or is found guilty of that offence, the Sheriff may order the child to be committed for such a period not exceeding two years as may be specified in the order to such a place as the Secretary of State may direct for the purpose of undergoing residential training and where such an order is made the child shall during that period be liable to be detained in that place subject to such conditions as the Secretary of State may direct.

Release on licence before the stated term, under the supervision of the child's social worker, however, is the responsibility of the Secretary of State and is based on reports from the residential establishment concerned and the relevant social work department. In the late 1970s in the school studied in this research most sentences lasted less than one year. Formal requests from headmasters for release are rarely refused if there is agreement between the residential establishment and social work department. (It should be noted that official figures in 1976-77 report the average length of stay to be 16 months when all List D schools are considered.)

For offences the Procurator Fiscal deems serious, Section 206(1) and (2) of the Criminal Procedure (Scotland) Act may be employed.

Section 206(1) of the Act states:

> A person convicted of murder who appears to the Court to have been under the age of eighteen years at the time of the murder shall not be sentenced to imprisonment for life: but in lieu thereof the Court shall (notwithstanding anything in this or any other Act) sentence him to be detained during Her Majesty's Pleasure, and if so sentenced he shall be liable to be detained in such place and under such conditions as the Secretary of State may direct.

Or Section 206(2):

> Where a child is convicted and the Court is of the opinion that none of the other methods of dealing with the child is suitable, the Court may sentence him to be detained for such a period as may be specified in the sentence: and where such a sentence has been passed the child shall during that period be liable to be detained in such a place and on such conditions as the Secretary of State may direct.

Section 206(1) cases are released at Her Majesty's Pleasure and the Secretary of State must approve such a decision.

For Section 206(2) cases release under remission can occur only after a meeting of the Parole Board to review the case. Moreover, the prognosis for the future differs as boys receiving such a sentence tend to remain longer in the school than Section 413 cases.

Figure 1.1 and Table 1.1 show the distribution of the committals of the boys in the Wing and Open school by the Hearings and the Courts.

Section 206(1): 'A person convicted of murder'

It is important to note that no Section 206(1) cases occur in either group. In Scotland at the moment of writing (October 1977) there were only three Section 206(1) cases of children under sixteen years (Fiddes, *Personal Communication*). One case is in another Scottish 'closed' unit, one in a young offenders institution and one in a detention centre. The Wing is innocent of children committed under Section 206(1). Murder by children is very rare, its occurrence being most remarkable and newsworthy when it does occur, as in the celebrated Mary Bell case. (Over the 17 years which the Wing has existed it has held only two boys who have killed.) (Imlach 1979)

Clearly none of the boys in our sample are involved in murder either in the Open school or in the Wing. This could be held as surprising in that, at least in the Wing, the public might suppose it to contain 'dangerous,

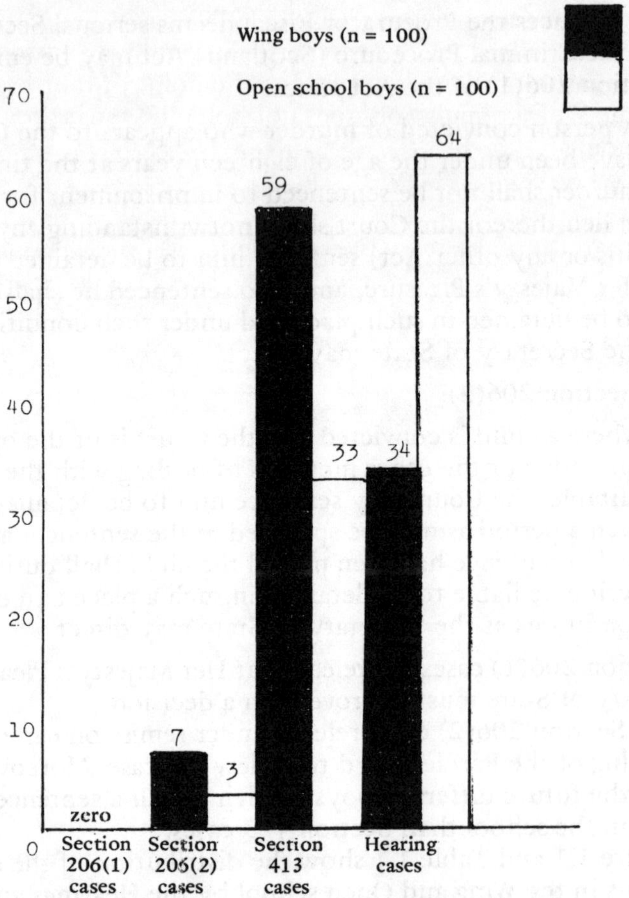

Figure 1.1 Committal of boys under Section 206(1), Section 206(2), Section 413 and Hearings

Table 1.1

Number of boys committed under Section 206(1), Section 206(2), Section 413 and Hearings

	Section 206(1) cases	Section 206(2) cases	Section 413 cases	Hearing cases
Wing (n = 100)	0	7	59	34
Open school (n = 100)	0	3	33	64

unruly and disruptive' boys. Clark (1979) has already pointed out that children can fall into such a category without being murderers. Nevertheless, the myth of 'dangerousness' to the point of murder in the secure unit (the Wing) population does not hold and must provide cause for reflection.

Table 1.2

Committal of boys in the Wing (n = 100) and in the Open school (n = 100) by Section 206(1), Section 206(2), Section 413 and Hearings

	Wing (n = 100)	Open school (n = 100)	Chi-square test of significant difference	Level of significance
Section 206(1)	0	0	–	–
Section 206(2)	7	3	x^2 = 1,6842, df = 1, $p > 0.10$	not significant
Section 413	59	33	x^2 = 13,6070, df = 1, $p < 0.001$	0.001 (very highly significant
Hearings	34	64	x^2 = 18,0072, df = 1, $p < 0.001$	0.001 (very highly significant)
TOTAL	100	100	–	–

Section 206(2)

This section has been used for seven boys in the Wing (7 per cent) and for three (3 per cent) in the Open school. This is not significantly different ($p > 0.10$) and could occur by chance. The different incidence does not therefore indicate that the offences of the secure unit boys are significantly more serious in numbers than in the Open school.

The total of ten Section 206(2) cases in the cohort of 200 per cent is small, yet, curiously, all serious cases are not committed under Section 206(2). For example, an assault which would appear 'grave', a boy hitting another in the eye with a billiard ball and blinding him permanently, was dealt with by a Hearing; while another who resisted arrest in a melée of youngsters and police while in a football crowd in the streets of Perth was committed under a Section 206(2) disposal (police assault). Incidentally the boy's emotional state was not considered in any way mitigatory by the Court although he had been disturbed that morning by his mother's marriage to a man he strongly resented, and had been drinking after the wedding party. Nor was the policeman in any way injured. Moreover, this boy had no previous convictions of any kind.

Morris and McIzaac seriously question the rationale for ascribing children to different disposals (Morris and McIzaac 1978). In a comparison between the procedure in two regions of Scotland, they observe enormous differences, depending (they write) on the subjective opinions in the officials concerned, not on law. The social values of social workers, police, reporters and procurator fiscals are all varied and children are submitted to these apparently at random. Children in List D schools are probably more aware of these differences than any other group, in that they compare with each other their own experiences of the law.

Section 413

In the Wing 59 per cent of boys are sentenced under Section 413 of the Criminal Procedure (Scotland) Act 1975. Only 33 per cent of the Open school boys lie under this order. The significant difference observed implies that the offences of the Wing boys are considered more serious than those of the Hearing boys.

As has been said above, a Section 413 sentence is for 'not exceeding two years' but generally boys spend about ten months of this sentence, in parallel with the ten months' training now served in Borstal. A boy can serve the full extent of his sentence but most schools now reduce this, using it implicitly as a sanction. The knowledge the boys have that 'good behaviour' reduces their time is an important mode of controlling behaviour. Schools find this a useful, if unexpressed help, in working with their boys.

'Getting their date' for all the boys is a continuing anxiety. No one has a certainty of when release will occur, neither the Section 206(2), the Section 413, nor the Hearing boys. They can estimate but can never know. They lie under a sword hanging by a thread.

Hearing cases

An almost inverse relationship obtains in the ratio between the Open school boys and the Wing boys. 64 per cent of Open school boys are from Hearings as opposed to 34 per cent of Wing boys. The minor difference between the groups is due to the Section 206(2) boys (see Table 1.2).

The influence of sentencing in prognosis

The Rushforth report found little statistical difference between the facts in case histories of all three categories: Hearings, Section 413 and Section 206(2) (Rushforth 1978). A 'halo' effect, however, was found in that staff regarded the boys differently, believing the 206(2) boys more 'criminal' than those in Section 413 and they in turn 'worse' than Hearing cases. Rushforth formed the view that types of sentencing appears not to be derived from reason but from chance. The boys, their background and their offences are very similar. Moreover, the decisions reached concerning the boys' disposal also appear random, for one boy may be released after an offence for which another boy might receive two years. However, once sentenced, the boy's future appears predetermined by the sentence. The progress (she found) towards further recidivist crime after release was more definite for the 206(2) boys, possibly due to their own self-image, derived from the 206(2) sentencing as 'hard men', and from the stereotypes into which they are cast by staff and other boys in the institution.

This falls into the 'labelling' theory recognised by Schur whereby boys fulfil the expectations laid on them following their convictions (Schur 1971). Taylor, Walton and Young (1973) in their comprehensive study of the literature of criminology, past and present, European and American, develop this theme. Its relevance to the present study is of importance.

Social influence of sentencing in the schools

In the school also, both the Open school and the Wing, the social hierarchy of power among the boys derives in some measure from the above disposals. 'Hearings' boys tend to be at the bottom of the pecking order and are liable to be teased or bullied if young or weak by boys established in the school on arrival. Homesickness, always acute on entry, is accentuated by the initiation processes. In the large Open school where numbers can amount to 80 or 90 boys this is always a problem as a covert proceeding and difficult for the staff to control or even detect. In the Wing with small numbers, rarely exceeding 25 boys, the problem hardly arises as staff ratio is high and boys are rarely if ever left alone and exposed to peer pressures.

By contrast, Section 413 boys are not seen by the other boys as equally vulnerable. They tend to have the charisma of 'hard men' ascribed to them and are already fulfilling the prophecy observed in 'labelling' theory. They begin to exaggerate the seriousness of their offences in their talk with other boys, boasting of deeds they may or may not have committed, taking on the chameleon role the sub-culture of the school appears to them to require, thus attaining prestige among their fellows.

Section 206(2) boys, three in the Open school and seven in the Wing, are ascribed an even greater bravura by the other boys, as well as by the staff, which may well surprise them after their experience in the Court. The gravity accorded by the Sheriff to their offence gives them paradoxical 'kudos' in the compulsory residential establishment. Their mild behaviour to staff and boys is admired (for they nearly all are gentle and even fearful boys) and seen as implicit strength. They come, as it were, into a more sheltered environment than the defenceless Hearings boys.

The above observations are drawn from close knowledge of the boys and the culture pattern of the school by personal experience over four years as a psychologist and from communications with staff, both senior and junior, of long and short experience.

Figure 1.1 and Table 1.2 appear to show that the boys in the Wing are more criminal than those in the Open school in that there are more Section 206(2) cases (though not significantly more), and more Section 413 cases. The next chapter analyses their offences in order to examine this hypothesis critically.

Summary

Two groups of 100 consecutive cases of boys each were selected for study, one from an 'open' List D school and one from a high security unit. Sources of committal are discussed, the Hearings and the Sheriff Court and the methods of conviction.

More boys from the Hearings are in the 'open' school and more boys from the Court in the high security unit. No cases of grave crime Section 206(1) occur in either group.

The effect of 'labelling' subsequent to sentencing is mentioned.

2 Offences

It might have appeared from Figure 1.1 and Table 1.1 that the boys in the Wing are more criminal than those in the Open school in that there are more Section 413 and Section 206(2) cases. Table 2.1, showing causes of disposal, gives the distribution in the Open school and the Wing and tends to modify this view.

Analysis of Table 2.1 shows clearly that there are no significant differences between the offences which cannot be ascribed to chance between the secure Wing boys and the Open school boys save in 'failure to attend school without reasonable excuse'. The Social Work (Scotland) Act 1968 Section 32(f) lays this down as a condition for 'compulsory measures of care' though this is rarely the only reason for an appearance at a Hearing. Here, curiously, the Open school boys show a greater incidence of school refusal at a highly significant level. This finding will be discussed further later. In all other offences the two groups are homogeneous.

Absconding and previous placements

When the case files are searched it emerges that the main difference between the two groups lies in the fact that the Wing boys have persistently absconded from previous placements to which the authorities have allocated them and have significantly more previous placements. Absconding, through 'failing to meet the requirements of the establishment' as ordered is not a primary offence. It is a consequence of 'treatment' and deriving from that 'treatment'. It indicates that the boys are not content with the placement and flee, thus silently giving evidence of unhappiness. However, since all absconding is not noted in boys' files and numbers of flights cannot be counted with certainty, the number of previous placements constitute 'harder' data with persistent absconding noted.

Table 2.2 shows the comparative differences between the two groups of boys. In particular it shows vividly the two differences (highly significant at the 0.001 level in both instances) between the boys, and the importance of this data cannot be over emphasised when considering the two groups. Figure 2.1 and Table 2.3 show the previous placements of the boys in both groups. Mere inspection, confirmed by analysis by 't' test, shows that the two groups have highly significant differences

Table 2.1

Comparative analysis of offences

Offence	Wing	Open school	Chi-square test	Level of significance
Section 206(1)				
1 Murder and culpable homicide	0	0	–	–
Section 206(2)				
2 Rape, attempted murder, assault and robbery with firearms	0	0	–	–
3 Theft, housebreaking, opening lockfast premises	94	89	$x^2 = 1.2281$, df = 1, $p > 0.10$	not significant
4 Car theft, Road Traffic Act offences and theft	37	25	$x^2 = 1.108$, df = 1, $p > 0.10$	not significant
5 Car theft without other offences	0	4		not significant
6 Assault	10	15	$x^2 = 1.428$, df = 1, $p > 0.10$	not significant
7 Fire-raising*	3	3	–	–
8 Carrying offensive weapons*	3	2	–	–
9 Sex offences*	1	2	–	–
10 Drug offences*	0	0	–	–
11 Glue-sniffing* (not illegal)	3	4	–	–
12 Failure to attend school, exclusion	57	76	$x^2 = 8.1023$, df = 1 $0.01 > p > 0.001$	0.001 (highly significant)

*These offences are not appropriate for comparison by the chi-square test of significant difference or even by the Mann–Whitney U test, being less than ten cases each.

Table 2.2

Absconding and previous placements

	Wing	Open school	Chi-square test	Level of significance
Persistent absconding from previous placements.	87	13	$x^2 = 109.52$, df = 1, $0.001 > p$	0.001 (very highly significant)
Three or more previous placements	77	20	$x^2 = 62.78$, df = 1, $0.001 > p$	0.001 (very highly significant)

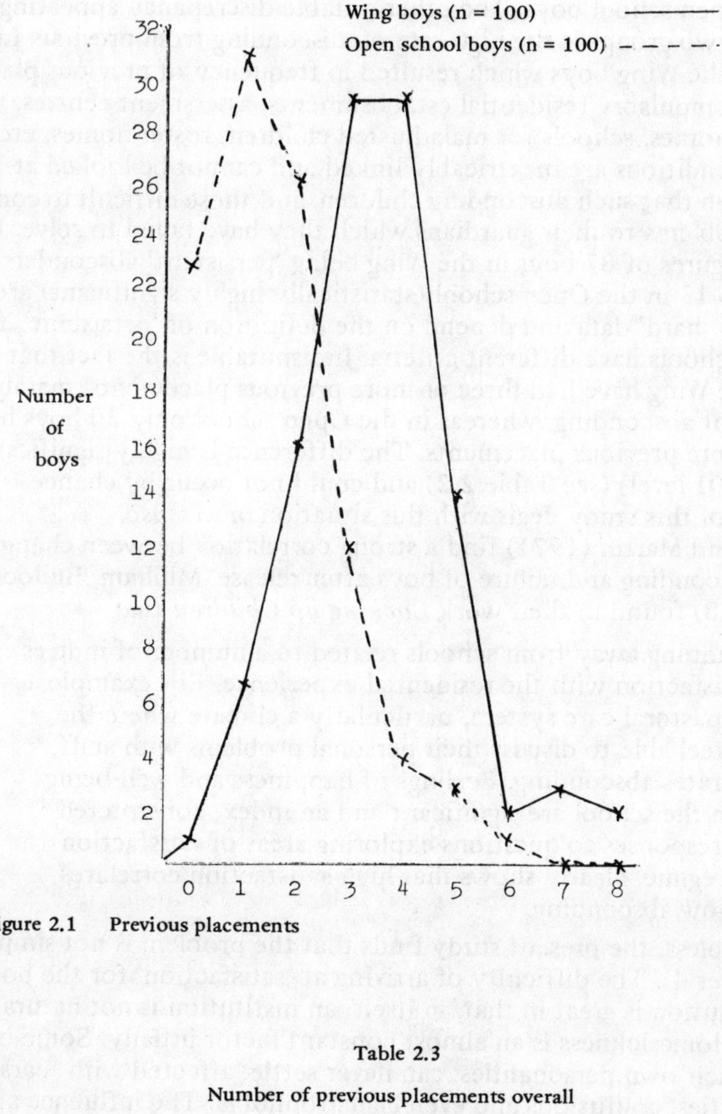

Figure 2.1 Previous placements

Table 2.3

Number of previous placements overall

Number of previous placements	0	1	2	3	4	5	6	7	8	
Wing boys (n = 100)	0	7	16	28	28	14	2	3	2	77 placements of 3 or more
Open school boys (n = 100)	23	31	26	12	4	3	1	0	0	20 placements of 3 or more

't' = 9.9, df = 198, $p < 0.001$ (highly significant)

between the means. The Wing boys have many more previous placements than the Open school boys. The other notable discrepancy appearing between the two groups is the high rate of absconding from previous List D schools in the Wing boys which resulted in frequency of previous placements in compulsory residential establishments, assessment centres, childrens' homes, schools for maladjusted children, foster homes, etc. The two conditions are inextricably linked and cannot be looked at separately in that such absconding children, and those difficult to contain, present problems to their guardians which they have failed to solve. However, the figures of 87 boys in the Wing being 'persistent' absconders as opposed to 13 in the Open school (statistically highly significant) are not completely 'hard' data and depend on the definition of 'persistent', for different schools have different criteria. Indisputable is the fact that 77 boys in the Wing have had three or more previous placements, mainly due to persistent absconding, whereas in the Open school only 20 boys have three or more previous placements. The difference is highly significant (at the 0.001 level) (see Table 2.2) and could not occur by chance. Chapter 4 of this study deals with this situation *in extenso.*

Clarke and Martin (1971) find a strong correlation between changes of school, absconding and failure of boys after release. Millham, Bullock and Hosie (1978) found in their work *Locking up Children* that

> . . . running away from schools related to a number of indices of satisfaction with the residential experience. For example a good pastoral care system, particularly a climate where the boys feel able to discuss their personal problems with staff, moderates absconding. Feelings of happiness and well-being within the school are significant and an index, constructed from responses to questions exploring areas of satisfaction with regime, clearly shows that high satisfaction correlates with low absconding.

Nevertheless, the present study finds that the problem is not simple (see Chapter 4). The difficulty of arriving at 'satisfaction' for the boys in an institution is great in that, in itself, an institution is not natural for children. Homesickness is an almost constant factor intially. Some boys, through their own personalities, can never settle, affected with fears, with anxieties, confusions and even claustrophobia. The influence also of unhappy previous placements is not easily changed.

In all, therefore, the most highly significant difference between the two groups of boys in the Wing and the Open school lies in the level of previous placements and abscondings. Absconding is not in itself an offence against the law but it is to the institution. The boys in the Wing, in high security, demonstrate this. Millham, Bullock and Hosie (1978) write trenchantly, giving the findings of their own research:

> The more we allow security to be seen as the answer to absconding the more we obscure what all research demonstrates: *that it is the nature of the child's residential experience that makes him an absconder, that boys run because of the places they are in.*

(The italics are theirs.)

The offences

It is important to note how low the level of the offences of the boys actually is, apart from those of theft in which nearly all the boys in both groups are convicted (see Table 2.1). The offences are against property, obviously a matter of extreme concern to our society in that thieving children are placed in segregation in consequence. It is clear too from the same table that offences against persons are low in both groups, although slightly higher (not statistically significant) in the Open school group.

Discussion of each of the categories of offences in Table 2.1 now follows, for a stark catalogue masks the variety and drama of the boys' experiences and the seemingly haphazard events which succeed on each other leading eventually to the hearings and courts.

1 and 2. Section 206(1)—murder and serious crime

The fact that no Section 206(1) disposals occur in either group and not even in the Wing is of interest in dispelling the myth that boys in high security units are 'dangerous' and have committed acts of serious violence. It would be possible to hold a boy for such offences in the Wing but as has been said above such offences are very rare.

Section 206(2)—no rape, attempted murder, or assault and robbery with firearms occurred in the cases in this study (serious crime). The ten boys (see Figure 1.1) sentenced under Section 206(2) had offences similar to the Section 413 boys.

3. Theft, housebreaking, opening lockfast premises (mainly dealt with by the Hearings)

Nearly all the boys in both groups are involved in theft either of property or cars and sometimes of both. The difference between the groups is not statistically significant (see Table 2.1). Offences listed in this table can be ancilliary so that few categories are exclusive of any other. Precise calculation is thus possible only for types of offence, the offenders sometimes having theft, and car theft, failure to attend school, absconding or assault.

Theft, so widely disseminated, covers a variety of acts from little boys commencing their careers of crime with stealing sweets and cigarettes to those who steal cars. The nature of the thefts tends to be underemphasised, for once guilt has been admitted there appears little differential in punishment for different acts, the theft of a large sum of money ranking with minor sums. Indeed the amount stolen is usually a matter of what is available by chance, a bonanza or a few pence. Morris and McIsaac found the average value of goods stolen by children to be around £25. Few offences are planned with a knowledge of what is sought. 'Going robbing' can be fun for small groups of boys looking for diversion and mischief in urban surroundings just as bird-nesting or fishing would occupy country boys. One boy described his pleasure in entering a house 'like Aladdin's cave' where like Aladdin he could, as a thief, take anything he chose. The excitement and danger, as in Aladdin's case, sharpened his delight. Curiosity also as to how other people live is part of this activity combined with the thrill of the forbidden.

Stolen goods or money are quickly squandered as being 'worthless', often wasted in fairgrounds and by 'treating' other children recklessly until the money is spent. Perhaps in this way the guilt of theft is considered expiated, for most thieving children know stealing is wrong, and are aggressively protective of their own property.

It is well known that police complain that the carelessness of the public concerning property provokes much juvenile crime, for example leaving seductive articles in unlocked cars, for most theft is accidental, occurring when temptation and opportunity coincide. Few of the boys consider themselves as professionals, planning and executing burglaries. Shoplifting is also mostly impulsive. The few children in the study recognised by MacIntosh (1971) as being trained as skilled thieves by their families are egregious in the school studied in this research and considered 'odd' by the main body of boys. Nevertheless, casual theft is endemic as it is throughout our society, laws crystallising the ways it is controlled. People want to keep what they have, as much as they want to increase what they own but the parameters of propriety in so doing are less definite than is generally supposed. 'White collar' crime (Reiss 1979) is evidence of this.

Belson (1975), in an important study commissioned by the Home Office, investigated stealing in London boys, drawing a representative sample from the general population, not from a sample of detected thieves. In this enquiry 1,429 boys were asked through a procedure called the 'elicitation technique' for information about whether or not they had ever committed various types of theft, of which 44 types were listed. He found:

> It is clear that stealing by boys is well spread throughout the different social sectors of the London population, with a clear tendency for involvement in theft to increase as we go down the parental occupational scale. Nevertheless this tendency is not maintained for those in the *bottom* occupational group (the sons of the unskilled), their theft level being lower than that for the semi-skilled. . . . no class of theft of the forty-

> types listed was endorsed by less than five per cent of boys. In general the percentages of boys admitting ever committing the different types of theft was high, e.g. eighty-eight per cent had at some time stolen something from school; seventy per cent had at some time stolen something from a shop; thirty-three per cent from a stall or barrow; thirty per cent had at some time got something by threatening others; twenty-five per cent had stolen from a car, lorry or van; eighteen per cent had stolen from a telephone box; seventeen per cent letters or parcels; eleven per cent from a meter; five per cent had taken a car, a lorry or a van. The average of such percentages *for all forty-four types of theft* was forty-two per cent. With the discounting of thefts involving trivia the overall average stands at thirty per cent.

The evidence Belson gathered was from boys between thirteen and sixteen years old, in a sophisticated procedure designed to ensure truthfulness and trust so that their evidence was presumed reliable. Boys were given promises of anonymity and with firm assurances that nothing they had revealed would be connected with them personally.

Belson clearly found that stealing is widespread in all social classes

> with the sons of the professional sector quite substantially involved in stealing. The position is broadly similar with respect to school background: boys with secondary modern or comprehensive schooling are more involved than boys with grammar school or public school backgrounds but even the latter are quite substantially involved in stealing (op.cit. p.87).

This tacit double standard of honesty clearly exists also among adults. Tax avoidance and tax evasion are clearly linked. Expense accounts are a grey area with some professionals. Social agreement decides on a varying personal scale what is 'allowable'. Language uses euphemisms with delicate shades of meaning for dubious activities, stealing, borrowing, winning, nicking, screwing, lifting. The taking of money is always seen as outright and recognisable theft, and is often justified in the thief's own view because it allows him momentarily to improve his lifestyle. Alcohol, food, records, transistors and clothes are other such targets. In the last two decades the criminologists have developed a body of philosophic thought on crime. (For a critique, see Taylor, Walton and Young 1973.) American sociologists, fascinated by social contemporary patterns, suggest that deviance and delinquency occur when society's rules have degenerated into anomie so that laws do not carry weight. For the ambitious underprivileged the ends justify the means since they cannot achieve what they wish legally. Thus gangsters are socially accepted once they have become rich, the financial success of their labours legitimising their crimes in the eyes of other Americans (Taylor, Walton and Young 1973, Matza 1964, Lemert 1967, Cohen 1971, Cloward and Ohlin 1960). In our society, in a different culture, theft is despised but continues, a precarious balance being maintained. The boys in our study are the ones who have been 'caught' yet all will admit that many of their offences have occurred without detection.

All in all it is recognised by the boys that their thieving is not a 'one off' occurrence. The first offence may receive 'no action' when the charge from the Police reaches the Reporter, a letter being sent to the family with a warning. A further charge may lead to a formal Police warning. Later, as offences accrue, a Hearing may be called and the child put on voluntary or compulsory supervision to a social worker. It is not true, however, that childrens' Hearings apply a tariff system, for Hearing decisions are taken in the best interests of the child and not the number of offences committed overall.

Ancilliary to the actual offence the social enquiry report on the child and his family is carefully considered by the Hearing. If the Hearing judges that the parents are capable and caring of their child 'compulsory' action is seldom taken (Finlayson 1976). Only if the parents are seen as incompetent does the state intervene. Thus the underprivileged and neglected child has a different outcome to the fortunate and well brought up. It will be seen later in this study (Chapter 3) how the families of the boys in the cohort rate in this regard. Burstall's (1979) Matthew Effect flourishes here: 'For unto everyone that hath shall be given and he shall have abundance: but from him that hath not shall be taken away even that which he hath'.

The Hearing comes eventually as a formal intervention for persistently deviant children, endeavouring to advise families concerning their child. There is, however, a need to study why in some regions or parts of regions a higher proportion than would be expected of children in trouble find their way before the Courts, or that most theft offences to to the Hearings.

Analysis of the interval between the first Hearing and the compulsory residential placements here studied now follows.

Figure 2.2 and Table 2.4 show the length of time since the first Hearing of the boys and their admission to the Forest School. It is clear that the Open school boys have been involved in offences for less time than the Wing boys.

Statistical analysis reveals a real difference between the two groups of boys in the length of their involvement with the law since their first offence (see Figure 2.2). Eleven Open school boys had their first Hearing in the year they came to the Forest School. Only one Wing boy has the same story, a boy who had initially been placed in the Open school and went on hunger strike. He remained for only a few

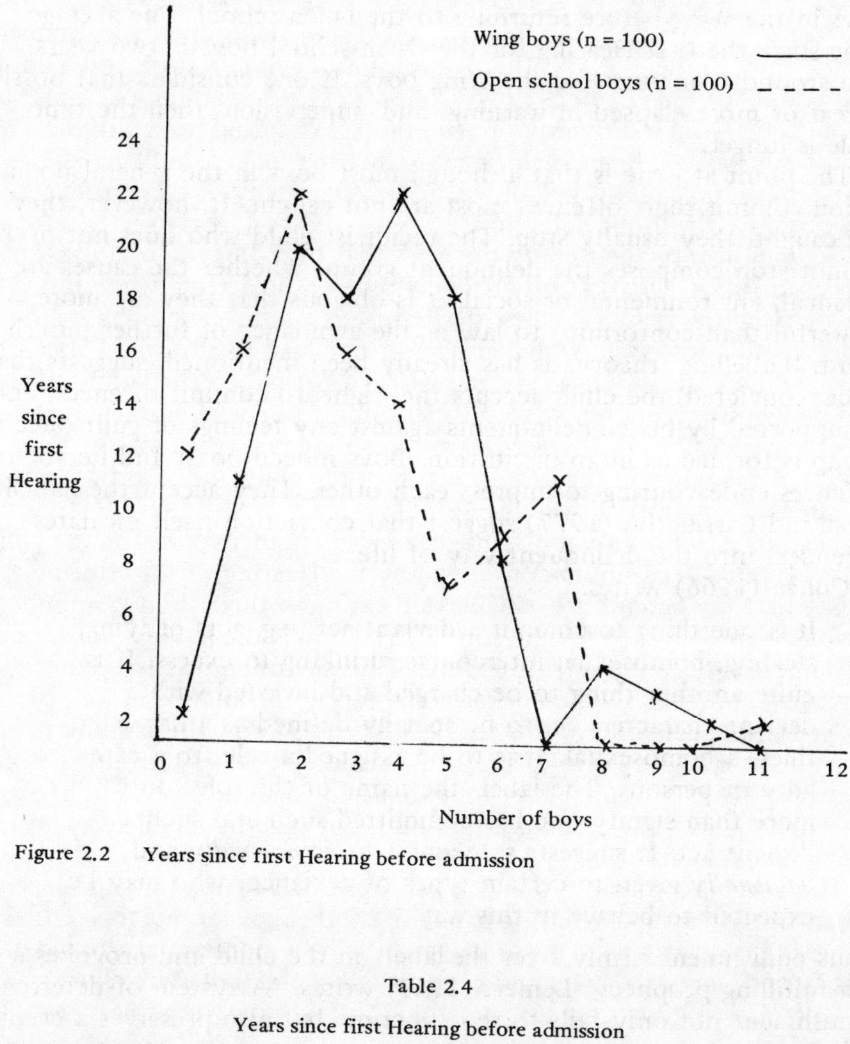

Figure 2.2 Years since first Hearing before admission

Table 2.4

Years since first Hearing before admission

Years since first Hearing	0	1	2	3	4	5	6	7	8	9	10	11	12
Wing boys (n = 100)	1	10	19	17	23	17	7	0	3	2	1	0	0
Open school boys (n = 100)	11	15	21	15	13	6	8	10	0	0	0	1	0

't' = 2.30, df = 198, $0.05 > p > 0.10$ (significant difference)

days in the Wing before returning to the Open school. The average time since the first Hearing for the Open school boys is two years, and around four years for the Wing boys. If one considers that possibly a year or more elapsed in warnings and 'supervision' then the time scale is longer.

The point at issue is that although most boys in the general population commit theft offences most are not caught. If, however, they are caught, they usually stop. The recidivist child who does not or cannot stop composes the delinquent group. Whether the causes are personal, environmental or social, it is obvious that they are more powerful than conformity to law or the avoidance of further punishment. 'Labelling' theory, as has already been mentioned, suggests that once 'convicted' the child accepts the 'right' to commit offences, and is supported by his co-delinquents against any feelings of guilt once a group is formed as in an institution. Boys indeed boast and lie about offences endeavouring to impress each other. They accept the 'labelling'. West and Farrington (1977) suggest that conviction itself escalates offenders into the delinquent way of life.

Cohen (1966) writes:

> It is one thing to commit a deviant act, e.g. acts of lying, stealing, homosexual intercourse, drinking to excess. It is quite another thing to be charged and invested with a deviant character, i.e. to be socially defined as a liar, a thief, a homosexual. It is to be assigned a role, to a category of persons. The label—the name of the role—does more than signify one has committed such and such a deviant act. It suggests someone who is *normally* and *habitually* given to certain types of deviance: who may be expected to behave in this way.

Thus punishment firmly fixes the label on the child and provokes a self-fulfilling prophecy. Lemert (1967) writes: 'A system of deterrent punishment not only fails to repress crime but also preserves a criminal class'.

Walter and Jones (1978) follow these thoughts from a slightly different angle. 'Delinquency is fun.' They comment that:

> Delinquent activity is considered in Social Work theory to be the result of personal deprivation, usually believed to have started in a disordered family which is then exacerbated by a whole range of factors such as poor housing, poorly staffed schools, poor employment prospects and so on, with which the child cannot cope because of deficiencies in his early years. Much research has confirmed these findings . . . Yet the boys themselves have a rather

> different view.
>
> What middle-class adults call delinquency the boys themselves see as fun. What they are concerned with is whether an activity is fun: whether it is legal is another matter. To them what makes an activity legitimate is that it is enjoyable. In this the boys are influenced by the cultural norms of our society which say that childhood is a time when fun, games, and play are positively good. Yet access to socially approved fun is unevenly distributed among the social classes and in different areas. Many of the means that enable other children to have fun—holidays, large suburban gardens and playgrounds—are often not available to those who end up in the delinquency statistics. For them the excitement and variety of the street is the most accessible avenue for having fun and this means playing with public property belonging to strangers and it means playing with or at the cost of members of the public. Risking getting caught is all part of the excitement. Whereas fun involves taking hold of life (what Matza calls the mood of humanism), getting caught is a matter of fate catching up with you (the mood of fatalism) . . . The kid sees fun and excitement not as a *problem* to be explained and treated by social work therapy but as a totally normal part of life. He is puzzled when a magistrate or social worker asks him to attempt an explanation for his getting into trouble. Why, he asks himself, do they want an explanation for something which is everyday and normal? . . . If life for the delinquent is a continuous experience of avenues of fun being closed off then 'getting sent away' is the ultimate in this process, for it closes all avenues off. Whereas for those like the Police and social workers 'trouble' is the fun the kid was up to, for the kid 'trouble' is getting caught and sent away.

Walter and Jones' view is facile but corrective to extravagant claims that social circumstance causes delinquency. Rather it is a correlative, pointing to the vitality and energy of the children in adverse living circumstances.

Nevertheless, all boys in deprived areas do not commit offences to the extent of 'being sent away'. One child's reproachful protest in defence of his home territory should be remembered. 'There are good folks in Drumchapel!' (Drumchapel is an area of multiple deprivation in Glasgow.)

In summary, theft is the largest common factor in bringing boys into the compulsory residential setting. The difference in numbers between the boys in the Wing and the Open school is not statistically significant and could arise through chance.

Boys in the Wing have a longer time span since their first Hearing than the Open school boys.

4. *Car theft* (mostly dealt with by the Courts)

Table 2.1 shows that 37 boys in the Wing have charges of car theft, theft, and Road Traffic Act offences. 29 boys in the Open school have the same offences (four having only car theft charges). However, a chi-square analysis of difference fails to reach significance. The comparison here is between the number of boys falling into the *category* of Road Traffic Act offences. It was not possible to compare the *frequency* of these offences but it is the writer's understanding that the Wing boys commit these offences habitually as a transport convenience in absconding, whereas the Open school boys are more likely to commit the 'one off' offence. Road Traffic Act offences are dealt with by the Sheriff Court, sometimes with a recommendation for secure accommodation, attracting Section 413 sentences, especially for multiple offences over a short period. Disqualification of a driving licence may be incurred and this can only be imposed by a Court.

In one region such cases are often not dealt with by the Court but by the Hearings as the result of close liaison between the Reporter and Procurator Fiscal (Finlayson 1976). One Edinburgh boy in the Wing with well over 30 charges of car theft has not been disqualified. Generally, however, throughout Scotland the Courts deal with Road Traffic Act offences.

Therefore, at the Court stage, it may be that the 'needs of the child' and 'what is the child's best interests' are not so powerful in effecting decisions. The Court deals with facts, guilty or not guilty, even with mitigation. There is, of course, the fact that if an order is made under Section 413 or Section 206(1) or (2) of the Criminal Procedure Act (Scotland) 1975 that when actual placings occur the files are scrutinised by officials within Social Work Services Group who can and do call for additional information as appropriate and no doubt form decisions with the child's best interests in view.

Thus, in the case of car theft in the under sixteens the nature of the offence counts, not only its gravity. The frequency of car theft in the Wing boys is related to the frequency of their absconding (see Table 2.2) in that they take cars for transport in evading capture and returning home. Some boys are skilful and careful drivers and little harm is done to the car when it is finally abandoned, save for the nuisance caused to its owner. Courts, however, view car theft as a dangerous and vicious offence because some boys drive dangerously and accidents do occur, causing damage to the public and themselves.

There are no statistics for this, but one bad accident creates a general belief that *all* stolen cars are driven dangerously. Many people on reflection would prefer to have their car 'borrowed' than their home entered and searched for booty, in that the former offence is less personally disturbing. The boys themselves see car theft as more 'honourable' than other offences and differentiate between cars stolen from garages (impersonal) and those from private owners. Car theft to them has more style than housebreaking and brings them more prestige in the school itself. There is no 'profit' motive. They pride themselves on this distinction and indeed have a charisma which the other boys acknowledge. However, if the car theft is associated with other behaviours, prestige evaporates. A very few boys have no other offences (see Table 2.1) and tend to be regarded as aristocrats of the school by the boys. In the cohort studied there were four such boys in the Open school and none in the Wing—boys joyriding and on their first conviction.

The Wing boys, with a trend towards more car offences, have their charges contaminated by other thefts. As has been said above, in cases of absconding, living rough, and between and during various placements charges of theft inevitably accumulate. Unlike the Open school boys, the Wing boys have not been living at home, cared for by parents, fed and clothed and stealing cars merely for diversion.

It is undoubted that some boys are fascinated by cars. They learn to drive on wasteland either in their parents' cars or their friends'. The urge to get on the road eventually overwhelms them, and the law is broken. Often, when learning, they become very knowledgeable concerning the machine, entranced by its magic. Boys indeed regard cars with considerable awe, symbols of much they are denied by youth and poverty, and this leads to 'grabbing' what they cannot achieve legally (Lemert 1967). Psychoanalytically the car can be regarded as a symbol of sexual power. Girls are impressed by a boy with a car, sometimes particularly if they know it is stolen. Cars are stolen after parties for transport for an easy journey home and for sexual dalliance. It is part of the image the boy wishes to display in self-aggrandisement. Moreover, the knowledge that the Court will deal with the offence without sympathy adds to its glamour. It is not 'kid stuff', however young the offender may be. Indeed some children in primary school hardly big enough to see over the driving wheel are persistent car thieves, regardless of retribution. They know their danger. Indeed among the boys there is a widely held myth that every Sheriff in Scotland has himself had a cherished daughter killed by a stolen car driven by a boy and so exacts the maximum penalty' 'If you're caught you've had it!'

From the point of view of the public things are very different. The car is the second most valuable item the private citizen possesses, next to his house, if he owns either. If on hire purchase it is equally valued. It is no wonder that retribution for car thieves is required by the public even if insurance covers the loss.

More objectively the boy breaks several laws designed to protect the citizen. He has no insurance, no licence, not even accepted training. In a more savage age horse thieves were hanged. Now they are liable to get a Section 413 or 206(2) sentence.

In summary, in considering car theft cases, it is proper to note that in the 200 cases examined only 66 cases, in aggregate, occur—slightly more than one quarter. From the 100 Wing boys there were 37 cases (slightly over one third) and from the 100 Open school boys 29 cases (slightly over one quarter) of whom four boys have no other type of charge.

6. *Assault*

Table 2.5

Nature of assault charges

	Victims	Assaults by Wing boys	Assaults by Open school boys	
a	Peers	5	4	n.s.
b	Family	0	4	n.s.
c	School teachers	1	2	n.s.
d	Police	2	1	n.s.
e	Adult female	0	2	n.s.
f	Strangers	1	1	n.s.
g	Assault on Social Worker	1	0	n.s.
h	Armed robbery (razor threat)	0	1	n.s.
	TOTAL	10	15	n.s.*

*A chi-square (goodness of fit) test shows this difference to be not significant ($x^2 = 1.0$, df = 1, $p > 0.10$).

Notes: The numbers in the other comparisons are too small for the chi-square test to be appropriate. Observation shows the closeness of incidence.

This offence has strong emotional connotations, old ladies mugged in the street, the evil boys of the 'Clockwork Orange', little girls with throats slit, a mythology of horror springs from the public press. Yet one such event can blacken a whole range of young people. In actual analysis in the cohort of 200 boys studied, there are 25 cases, 15 in the Open school and 10 in the Wing. This is not a significant difference statistically. But the weighting of numbers for violence inclines towards the Open school boys.

(a) *Peer assault* (9 cases, 5 in the Wing, 4 in the Open school). Examination of Table 2.5 shows that the majority of assault cases are in quarrels with peers. Some were quarrels in school playgrounds, some in gang fights in city areas where such behaviour is part of the adolescent culture pattern.

(b) *Family assault* (4 cases, 0 in the Wing, 4 in the Open school). One case was in a fight resisting assault from a drunken stepfather: one with a brother in a cinema: one with an older sister in a family quarrel: one with parents, both mother and father being attacked.

No cases occur in the Wing boys. This is possibly because Wing boys have suffered more compulsory residential placement than Open school boys; or possibly because they have more gentle natures; or possibly merely by chance.

(c) *School assault* (3 cases, 1 in the Wing, 2 in the Open school). Two cases of attacking teachers occur in the Open school and one in the Wing.

(d) *Police assault* (3 cases, 2 in the Wing, 1 in the Open school). The Wing boy was committed under a Section 206(2) disposal. The two Open school boys were dealt with by the Hearings.

(e) *Adult female assault* (2 cases in the Open school). One charge against a middle aged woman (not an old age pensioner) is described as follows by the boy. 'I was standing in the shop door when a fat old woman the worse for drink carrying a bag of empty bottles tried to pass and brushed against me. She was getting money on the empties for more booze. She shouted at me and I answered back. She then began hitting me with the bottles and went "aff the heid". She then went to the Police and charged me. Her friend who kept the shop went along with her blaming me.' The boy was indignant at the injustice. 'It should have been her who was charged!'

This story is quoted as against the emotional myths of old age pensioners assaulted by teenage thugs. It is the only instance in the 200 boys studied where an older woman is involved.

The other female assault is represented in the case of a

boy (John S.) who might well have been placed otherwise than in a List D school. The psychological report follows.

Psychological testing

Vernon graded word reading test:	reading age 7 years	
Wechsler intelligence scale for children	Verbal scale	IQ 84
	Performance scale	IQ 73
	Full scale	IQ 76
Gibson's spiral maze:	'Slowest and most careless of maladjusted boys' group'	
Kinetic family drawing:	unintelligent, rather uncontrolled five year old	
Rorschach:	limited but comparatively normal responses. Lacking creativity and shows little feeling.	

Report (7 July 1976)

This boy comes from a home where the mother has left the father and children, and is living elsewhere in the same town. Initially after her departure, the father, who was a turner in a carpenter's yard, looked after his boys who were four in number, assisted and advised by his own mother who lived in the vicinity. At Christmas this year however he became ill and the family went to live with his mother and thereupon the boys of this family alternated in their visits between the mother, father and the grandparents, and appear to be part of a reciprocal exchange of challenges between all three.

After the move to the grandparents' house truancy in all the boys became very high, although it had been present previously. The older boy, James, was of good intelligence but John appears to be bordering on mental handicap.

In appearance John is round-faced with full lips and eyes which blink and seem difficult for him to focus. His speech is confused and a coherent statement on any subject is very difficult for him to achieve. Several times during the interview he said that he was dizzy, and that he had forgotten things that happened only a short time previously. His school report carries the same picture in that his Headmaster says that he 'can get lost between classes and cannot be trusted to achieve any task without betraying erratic behaviour'. Difficulties, say this report, exist only to be evaded and truancy occurs when any problem arises in John's life in school.

John has always, it appears from the social enquiry report, been a child in delicate health. In infancy and until lately he has been subject to asthma. When aged ten he was knocked over by a car. In relating this John said that he remembered vividly waking up in the ambulance and that when he returned to school he found increasing difficulty with lessons which mounted to such an extent that truancy began. He said that previous to this accident he had enjoyed school and had attended. The suspicion occurs that there may have been brain damage sustained in this accident, although the social enquiry report says that the parents have denied that there was not total recovery.

John relates that after his mother left home life was not comfortable at home. His father came home from work and had to make the meal. The boys helped with tidying the house, but the father tended to be short-tempered and difficult. John conceived the idea of committing some offence so that he would be 'put away'. The social enquiry report and also a psychiatric report both confirm that John planned to commit an offence which would cause him to be removed from home. Initially he stole articles but was 'only given supervision'. He decided that something more serious was required and therefore the assault on the woman was perpetrated. In this it appears he approached this woman from behind and, he says, pretended to strangle her with a tie and, in the Police charge, there is mention of attempted rape. This second charge was not substantiated and John denies it strongly.

If this story is in fact true, he appears to have succeeded in his plan for he is now placed in the Forest School.

Bizarre thinking of this kind is most abnormal in its combined stupidity and cunning. The boy is over fifteen but his manner of thinking is that of a delinquent three year old.

It is strongly urged that the school doctor should be approached with the request that the boy should be investigated for brain damage by electro-encephalography. This does not appear to have been administered previously and would seem, at this stage, to be desirable.

Psychological testing discovered the Wechsler intelligence scale to be in the IQ 70–80 range, and the other tests (see above) bear out his poor intellectual functioning. John's learning both socially, intellectually and morally is at a low level. John is reading at below seven years reading age and his handwriting vestigial. It could be said merely that he knew that such a thing as writing existed, but little more. Comparison of John's school work before and after the accident would be informative in that loss of ability to write is often a concomitant and result of brain damage. It could be supposed that if John had been functioning at this low level throughout his primary school he would and should have been referred to special school. If deterioration did indeed occur after the accident, his truancy prevented school from realising the extent of the change.

The school report notes that John attracts sympathy by his pathetic helplessness on which he capitalises. The suggestion of selective brain injury presents itself strongly, his confusion and disintegrated talk reinforcing this view.

Recommendation

Referral to school doctor and further psychological surveillance.

Postscript: Shortly after release this boy reoffended and went for Borstal training.

(f) *Fights with strangers* (2 cases, 1 in the Wing, 1 in the Open school)

The Open school boy involved described the incident concerned graphically and, if his story is true, he and two friends were passing through a Glasgow alley when a drunk middle aged man swore at them and attacked them with an iron bar. In the ensuing melee the man was himself hurt badly and the group of boys charged and convicted.

Peter, the Wing boy who attacked a stranger, said in interview that throughout his childhood he had had attacks of gloom which made him withdraw from everybody around him, and made him unable to tolerate the presence of anybody near him. During these fits he used to withdraw from the family and from companions and come back late at night after the family had gone to bed to avoid talking to them. He was also overcome with feelings of intense aggression which he could not control. As he grew older these attacks of depression were accentuated if he was drinking, and on one occasion he had attacked a stranger and pushed him through a window without any provocation whatsoever. Peter felt that this was 'madness'. Throughout the interview and subsequently the boy was very melancholy. He was afraid of release which was to occur soon because he would then have to face the responsibility for his actions and the fits of strangeness. He repeatedly said he felt he wished to stay in the Carpenter Wing where he was safe. In the event his fears were justified for two years later Peter had been in Borstal and is now in prison.

(g) *Assault on social worker* (1case in the Wing)

The assault on a social worker occurred when the boy was absconding and the social worker attempted to restrain him.

(h) *Armed robbery* (1 case in the Open school—razor threat)

The psychological report here reproduced gives an account of this boy and his history.

Psychological testing

Neale analysis of reading ability:	reading age 8 years
Object relations test:	poverty of thought and no imaginative qualities, demonstrating low intelligence
Wechsler adult intelligence scale:	IQ 86

Report (26 March 1976)

Robert is a boy of rather low intelligence. He was convicted under Section 206(2) to eighteen months' detention on account of armed robbery. The offence occurred while he and a companion on leave from a List D school were under the influence of drink. They entered (he told me) a wine shop and threatened the Pakistani shop assistant with an open razor. Subsequently the lads fled, dropping the bottle of Bacardi which they had stolen, and were arrested. He was placed in Longriggend* and subsequently in the Forest School.

Robert is a pleasant faced youth with blonde hair. On the day he was interviewed he was newly back from the school mountain lodge, and was sunburned and in good spirits. He related that he had greatly enjoyed the lodge, the walks over the hills and the friendly atmosphere there between the boys and the staff.

Robert describes his offence with acute embarrassment, flushing angrily, but also ashamedly. Although this was not his first offence, the Forest School is his first compulsory residential placement. He is the eighth child in the family and, one suspects, its Benjamin.

His father is now in his mid-fifties and has been unemployed for many years. Robert does not know what his malady is, but says he has 'turns' and rarely leaves the house. Father is 'easy to get on with' and mother is 'kind'. In the family are eight children of whom three (according to the Social Enquiry Report) are mentally handicapped. The oldest, a stepbrother, is thirty-two, and a baker. Dougall (aged thirty) is suffering from lead poisoning, acquired due to working conditions as a demolition worker. Betty, aged twenty-eight, is mentally handicapped and never leaves the house. Samuel (twenty-six) works on the railway and so does Denis (aged twenty-four).

*A portion of Glasgow's prison for offenders under 21 and boys on an 'unruly certificate' on remand, or awaiting placement after sentence.

Denis (Social Enquiry Report) is mentally handicapped as is Donald (aged seventeen). Donald has been in a List D school, prison, and Longriggend. Robert, the youngest, appears to be the apple of his mother's eye.

Robert related that alcohol was forbidden in the house by his mother. His drinking before his offence, was a new experience to him. His companion, a 'wild' boy, had suggested the robbery.

During the interview Robert showed continual signs of anger. He accepted the interview but also resented it. The Social Enquiry Reports also describe his parents as 'hostile' in attitude and Robert is seen as 'unco-operative'. The psychiatrist who interviewed Robert in Longriggend gave the opinion that there were 'no signs of mental illness nor milder psychiatric abnormality about this boy. He impressed at first as being average intelligence'. In my interview with Robert also, the same observations obtained. The boy is a poor reader—reading age 8 years—and no assessment of handwriting or arithmetic was attempted as the boy showed obvious embarrassment. In the object relations test he showed considerable poverty in thought and no imaginative qualities of any kind. He could see no significance in the pictures and said so with resentment.

This is an angry antisocial lad, very sensitive to guilt on account of his offence. He flushes and shows shame at a level most unusual in List D boys.

Recommendation

No further psychological action as being counterproductive.

(Note: This Section 206(2) disposal did not involve firearms.)

Boys with assault charges alone. The cases of assault examined above are those of boys who have ancillary charges of theft. There are, however, boys in the Open school whose only charges are assault. As shown in Table 2.6 Wing boys with several placements all have other charges in addition to assault because of their various histories before and during placements.

Table 2.6

Boys with assault charges only

Nature of charge	Wing (n = 100)	Open school (n = 100)
Assault on adult man	0	1
Assault on brother in a cinema	0	1
Assault on peer	0	1

This table differs from Table 2.5 in that the boys had no charges other than assault, although included in the totals there: namely ten in the Wing and 15 in the Open school

The personal stories of the assault cases could encompass much space in this study. Sufficient is described, it is hoped, to reveal the stress the boys in some cases suffer. In other boys the quarrels with peers have themselves been lighthearted and injuries accidental though with severe retributive consequences for the boys themselves.

The number of assaults overall, for whatever cause, is small; 25 from the 200 boys in the cohort, i.e. 12½ per cent of the cases. It should be noted that more boys in the Open school (15) than in the Wing (10) have such charges although the difference is not significant statistically.

7. Fire raising (3 cases in the Open school, 3 cases in the Wing)

Fire raising is a curious event, inspiring fear in the mind of society. Analysis of the cases in this study minimises the anxiety in that most of the six cases are accidental. Of the three cases in the Open school one occurred when two ten year old boys were trying to rob a warehouse. Police were alerted and the boys made their way into the attic. In the darkness there they lit papers for torches which were dropped as they panicked. In the ensuing fire the boys were narrowly rescued by the Police. In the second case a boy, also very young, lit a fire in his classroom by setting the window curtains alight. The fire was discovered quickly and no major damage occurred. The boy was expelled and subsequently his delinquency developed into theft in the aimless schoolless days. The third boy was a witness while friends with whom he had stolen a lorry attempted to burn it to destroy the evidence. This lad was of low intelligence and low social adequacy.

The three cases in the Wing are very similar. One occurred when boys were robbing a chip shop and knocked over burning oil when disturbed by Police. The second was caused by youngsters starting a fire in a pile of empty cartons outside a shop, and the third by a child playing with matches in a barn.

None of these cases were the cause of the present placement of the boys, but had occurred in their past history as related in their dossier. The seeming non-intention of most of this fire raising is significant, occurring as a secondary consequence of other actions.

In summary, therefore, fire raising in this study appears accidental save in two cases.

8. Carrying offensive weapons

In Britain carrying offensive weapons is an indictable offence. Guns may not be carried save by licence. Chains, knives and knuckle dusters are forbidden. Boys nevertheless do carry the latter items in the urban areas of low socioeconomic status in Glasgow and other large cities where gangs of boys gather together and engage in territorial disputes. They are mainly of significance as threat but stabbing does occur, usually associated with alcohol. 'Grassing' by the victim does not happen so charges do not truly reflect the incidence. Boyle (1977) vividly describes this culture in his personal account of his Glasgow adolescence. Yet his embattled and dramatic account is significant in its singularity. Of the 200 cases under review in this study only five boys were charged with carrying offensive weapons, three in the Wing and two in the Open school. A Police body search which reveals a weapon involves an immediate serious charge. Alarming stories, which are exceptional, describe drunken fights with swords made of broken bottles (stabbing) of which little is later remembered, the victim escaping from hospital with the aid of his assailant to prevent charges being made on either side in friendly hangover pacificism. There is no mention of guns in any of the cases. The convictions for weapon carrying, therefore, are low and non-existent for guns.

9. Sex offences

Three only occur in the two groups of boys, two are in the Open school and one in the Wing. Two boys were charged with 'carnal knowledge' of underage girls, one Wing boy with a thirteen year old girl and another when 'on the run' and sheltered by the girl, his sweetheart. The mother discovered the boy in her daughter's bedroom, summoned the Police and he was arrested, after a fracas for which he was also charged for Police assault.

The third case (Open school) was of a boy who met his mother for the first time since infancy at the age of fifteen. He had been brought up by foster parents and discovered his mother with the aid of a sister, also recently found. It appears the mother had become a prostitute and an alcoholic and the boy's shock and distress changed him from a previously well behaved into a disturbed and delinquent boy. His offence was indecent exposure to an elderly female neighbour.

A further boy, not charged with a sexual offence, is described as 'openly masturbating in front of a female teacher'. He is in Forest Open school as 'being without parental control'.

10. Drug offences

None occur in either group.

11. Glue sniffing

Glue sniffing is at present not illegal, though Police, social workers and parents become alarmed because of its alleged 'dangerousness' and give grave warnings. It is, however, named in offences as an ancillary item. Children who are regular glue sniffers are usually unhappy and have a liability to incur 'chargeable' offences.

However, as the activity becomes more widespread among the young, anxiety appears to be diminishing concerning its dangers. Merrill (1978) appears to wish to defuse stress in adults over glue sniffing in children. She quotes Harriet Smith (1978) of the Pharmaceutical Research Foundation and Watson (1975) as 'being cautious about possible long term health effects'. It appears, as experience accumulates, that is is predominantly an activity of childhood which, barring accidents, is moderately harmless and non-addictive. Cases observed by the writer show roughness of facial skin due to the effects of the glue when inhaled from the potato-crisp bag in which it is sniffed, but otherwise the boys show no effects and express no withdrawal feelings when deprived of glue in the residential setting. Possible long term damage, as from tobacco, is of course not observable and is a matter for medical research.

In the present study only seven boys appear to have been involved, three in the Wing and four in the Open school. For them it provides an inexpensive 'kick' but when they can afford to buy alcohol they prefer it as more satisfying and also more 'adult'. Glue is for children, they say. Nevertheless, boys in the institution enjoy teasing staff, one might suspect, by sniffing at various domestic glues in the establishment—sometimes even petrol—exaggerating their 'high' for effect.

12. Failure to attend school and exclusion

The foregoing are offences, of various types, and may carry the burden of compulsory residential placement. But children can be placed in a List D school without charges and conviction for criminal behaviour if the Hearing believes them to be 'in need of compulsory measures of care' [Social Work (Scotland) Act 1968, Section 32(2)].

Table 2.7

Failure to attend school and exclusion

	Wing (n = 100)	Open school (n = 100)	Chi-square test	Level of significance
Failure to attend school	46	58	$x^2 = 2.8846$, df = 1, $0.10 > p > 0.05$	n.s. but a 'trend'
Exclusion from day school	11	18	$x^2 = 1.9762$, df = 1, $0.01 > p > 0.05$	n.s.
TOTAL	57	76	$x^2 = 7.86$, df = 1, $0.01 > p > 0.001$	0.001 (highly significant)

School difficulties loom large in the histories of both groups of boys. 133 boys from the cohort of 200 in both groups have 'failed to attend school without reasonable excuse', or have been excluded, as Table 2.7 shows. Psychologists working with school refusers know well that some such children are true school phobics whose problems are too deep for 'reason' (Kahn and Nursten 1968). Other children have as many 'reasons' as they are individuals but such reasons are not regarded as valid by their social workers or Hearings. The 'trend' for more school refusers to lie in the Open school group becomes highly significant when those who have been excluded from school are also counted. Some schools indeed exclude pupils from school because of truancy, a paradox the children recognise. In 1978 schools were requesting the right to exclude 'unsatisfactory' children as a means of maintaining their internal standards. The Pack Report (1977) resulting from an enquiry set up by the Scottish Education Department deals with this truancy and indiscipline in depth, suggesting, among other things, 'day' units and 'sanctuary' classes as methods of special care for such children. It is recognised that once out of school 'the devil finds mischief for idle hands' as the above figures for the many truant children in our study indicate.

The Act quoted above lists 'if he has failed to attend school regularly without reasonable excuse' as a condition for considering a child in need of compulsory measures of care (Section 32(2)f). This mandate lays a duty on Hearings which is uncomfortable to them, the child and the family. School phobic children can give 'no reasonable excuse' for phobia as this lies below the level of reason. A school chagrined by the child's failure to attend cannot in many cases comprehend the anguish of fear and withdrawal in the child's mind. It considers him in need of punishment not sympathy. Once referred to the panel, unless an educational psychologist or psychiatrist can intervene, the neurotic child, without any other offences, may well land in a compulsory residential institution. If he has had the bad luck to have even a minor offence and a 'deprived' family this oils the wheels for his disposal. The school phobic child, by reason of the Act, gets a rough deal (Kahn and Nursten 1968).

School reports always give advice to the Hearings and Courts on their pupils and hostile reports influence decisions on such children. Unhappily few if any List D children have commendations from their schools. 'Disruptive, aggressive, lying, cunning, bullying, dirty, unreliable' are the common appellations. Such schools deny responsibility to deviants. Friendly school reports retain children in the community, marshalling local resources patiently and kindly.

It is curious that more boys in the Open school appear to have had school difficulties than the Wing boys, but the probable explanation is that the Wing boys have been removed earlier from their home community and gone into the circuit of List D schools and so avoided normal schooling (see Figure 4.1). Warnock (1978) may in the future help such children.

In summary, more Open school boys have been school truants or excluded from school than Wing boys. This is probably due to their longer exposure to normal school in their community.

Non-offending boys

Only four boys, two in the Wing and two in the Open school, are in the Forest School and are without known offences (see Table 2.8).

Table 2.8

Non-offending boys

	Wing	Open school
Parental rejection, persistent absconding from several previous placements	1	0
Transfer from previous List D school, unruly behaviour and parental rejection	0	1
Family rejection	1	1
TOTAL	2	2

The Rushforth study (1978) in contrast finds a much higher number of non-offending children in List D schools in general. From Rushforth's sample of 268 boys:

> 65 were not offenders, (24 per cent). Of these 65 boys 26 were committed for truancy, 15 were beyond control of their parents, 8 were lacking parental control or in moral danger, and for 16 cases of non-offenders the reason for committal was omitted.

These causes are similar to those in the present study but the incidence much higher. It is indeed a conscious decision in the Forest School not to accept, save in exceptional cases, non-offending boys. Rushforth also found that seven of the non-offenders in List D schools fell into the category of 'socially disadvantaged' as defined in the National Children's Bureau study of the 1958 cohort of children (families with five or more children living in bad housing and with low income). She questions whether 'disadvantage . . . may unwittingly be compounded with other disadvantages by the agents of society and a child's life be progressively diminished'. The 'Matthew Effect' is indeed ever present.

In the four cases found in the present study, admission was perhaps not the most appropriate placement but a clear compromise. Certainly this reflects on the adequacy of other appropriate care for children in our community.

These four boys, two in each group, are boys whose families have ceased to extend care to them. The List D school received them because there was nowhere else for them. A report on Stephen (15+) is reproduced here to illustrate his story.

Psychological testing

Wechsler adult intelligence scale:	IQ 124
Vernon graded word reading test:	reading age 13 years
Arithmetic test age (WISC sub-test 3):	13 years
Handwriting:	neat and somewhat wavering
Rorschach:	disturbed personality

Report

Stephen is a brown haired boy with rather protruberant grey eyes and a pale face. He has an affectionate clinging nature and because of this he has endured considerable suffering. In the Forest School, however, he has had consistent and kindly counselling over his problems. His good intelligence, not yet deviant, may help him.

Stephen's main problem is that of separated parents. Both were Cornish. Their home after marriage was Coventry, but the father, being a long distance lorry driver, was far ranging. The couple separated when Stephen was seven years old. This schism brought distress to Stephen for he was attached to both parents. The father remarried and acquired a second family, and forgot about Stephen except when bothered by his importunate affection. Stephen, unable to believe this rejection, clung to his notion of a loving, caring father, in spite of contrary evidence, thus battering at a closed door.

His mother also had remarried in 1969. Stephen could not tolerate the new husband, probably from motives of jealousy. The new husband also found Stephen difficult; he, too, probably seeing Stephen as the product of an earlier sexual association of his new wife, was less than understanding of the lad. Deep family stress resulted and deviant behaviour from Stephen.

Stephen came to the Forest Open School and, after persistent absconding, was transferred to the Wing, in that it was obvious to the Headmaster that the lad would continue to abscond due to his anxiety state and desire to see his father.

Stephen's earlier history is even more sad. He was seven years old when his parents separated. The marriage had been stormy, the father unfaithful, drinking and violent to wife and children. Eventually he left with another woman, taking Stephen with him. The new home for the child was Lowestoft, where he attended primary school. Several moves appear to have occurred over the years thereafter. Father was given custody of Stephen at the divorce, but it appears the father was cruel to him and the mother charged the father with cruelty after seeing bruises on Stephen from the father's belt. She then regained custody. Returning at age thirteen to his mother's house, Stephen found a stepfather who also treated him strictly, and, it appears, unsympathetically.

The stepfather was strict and unfriendly with Stephen, keeping him in at night, and forbidding smoking. Stephen then began a pattern of running away. He was placed in two successive childrens' homes and eventually at about fifteen he made his way to Birmingham to find his natural father. He did not dare to contact his father directly but went to a house where his father had formerly lived with him. He broke into the house (which apparently was empty and uninhabited) and lived there until apprehended by the Police. The father was informed and visited Stephen in the local remand home where he scolded him, though not unkindly.

Stephen was sent back to Scotland and placed in an assessment centre, and after seven weeks came to the Forest School. The lad says he ran away from the Open school nine times before coming to the Wing.

In the Wing Stephen was initially much disturbed. He retains a glamorous picture of his father and gave a dreamlike story. He had helped his Dad on his lorry with food deliveries. They went fishing, played golf and darts and went walking each Sunday with the new wife. On Saturdays they both went together to football matches. This however does not appear to relate to actual facts.

The father appears to have rejected Stephen completely, and wanted nothing to do with him. He is, indeed, in his mother's custody legally so the father abrogates responsibility.

The problem was well understood in the Wing, and the Headmaster contacted Stephen's mother and stepfather, so that gradually the boy's unhappy position became clear to them. The stepfather wrote in a kindly way to Stephen, and both his mother and stepfather have visited him. Stephen now appears to accept his father's disappearance from his life, and has friendly and grateful feelings towards his stepfather. The stepfather has been active in arranging a job for Stephen on release, and offers him a home in friendly fashion. Stephen is surprisingly receptive to his overtures. He related to me that the stepfather was kind and thoughtful, and that possibly he, Stephen, had been much to blame when he was younger and did not get on with him.

The time in the Forest School has allowed Stephen and his family to grow toward reconciliation.

Recommendation

Stephen is leaving the Wing shortly. He should be counselled to maintain his new friendly relationship with his stepfather; and to accept that his father has other primary commitments; and to make his own life as an adult.

Postscript: Two years later Stephen has been in Borstal and also a young offenders' institution—the favourable prognosis for Stephen was in error.

Summary

From the preceding information on the offences of the boys it would seem that the myth that the Wing boys are more dangerous and difficult than the Open school boys does not hold. They have fewer cases of assault (although violence is low in both groups). They are no different in fire raising, weapon carrying, sex offences, drug offences and glue sniffing and both groups are very low in all these. Their theft level is not statistically different from that of the Open school boys, nor is the rate of car theft. The level of truancy and school exclusion is lower in the Wing group, although this may be explained by longer compulsory absence in residential care from normal school.

Wing boys are mainly different in that they have more previous placements and more absconding than the Open school boys, and have been longer in the care of the authorities. Perhaps they are showing less docility and conformity to incarceration, 'voting with their feet' against conditions disagreeable to them. The challenge they present to the establishments they thus reject ensures further 'secure accommodation' and so they come to the Wing. They are the Papillons (Charriere 1970).

3 Families

The family background of the boys is important as it bears on their history and development. Analysis provides the substantial data.

Size of family

The Wing boys (n = 100) come from families whose average size is 5.18 children, the range being 1 – 12 children – making 518 children in all.

The Open school boys (n = 100) come from families whose average size is slightly less, 4.79 children, with a range from 1 – 14,479 children in all. The difference between the groups is not significant.

The overall average for both groups is about five children, a total group of some 1,000 children. These larger figures compare with the national average family size of 1.9 children (Registrar General 1960) and are almost three times greater. The inverse relationship between family size and attainment has been shown by a number of workers (Douglas 1964, Nisbet and Entwistle 1967, and Davie, Butler and Goldstein 1972). The fact that the families in this study are so large is significant.

Figure 3.1 and Table 3.1 show the distribution. If the national average figures were plotted they would creep along the base at 1.9. It is of interest that the mode in the Wing is higher than in the Open school at five children but the Open school families, having a wider distribution, are not significantly different in size when exposed to analysis by 't' test.

Delinquent siblings

In the Open school group 37 boys have siblings who are in compulsory residential placement, either in List D schools or in Borstal. In the Wing group the number is higher at 45 boys. The difference is not significant ($x^2 = 1.01$, df = 1, $0.30 < p < 0.50$).

These figures are probably less than the actual number in that details of family events are not always known nor are they always available in the social enquiry reports of the boys. Police warnings were also unavailable for the present study.

Interviews with the boys reveal family patterns where older boys 'go robbing' with their little brothers. The younger boy will be helped through

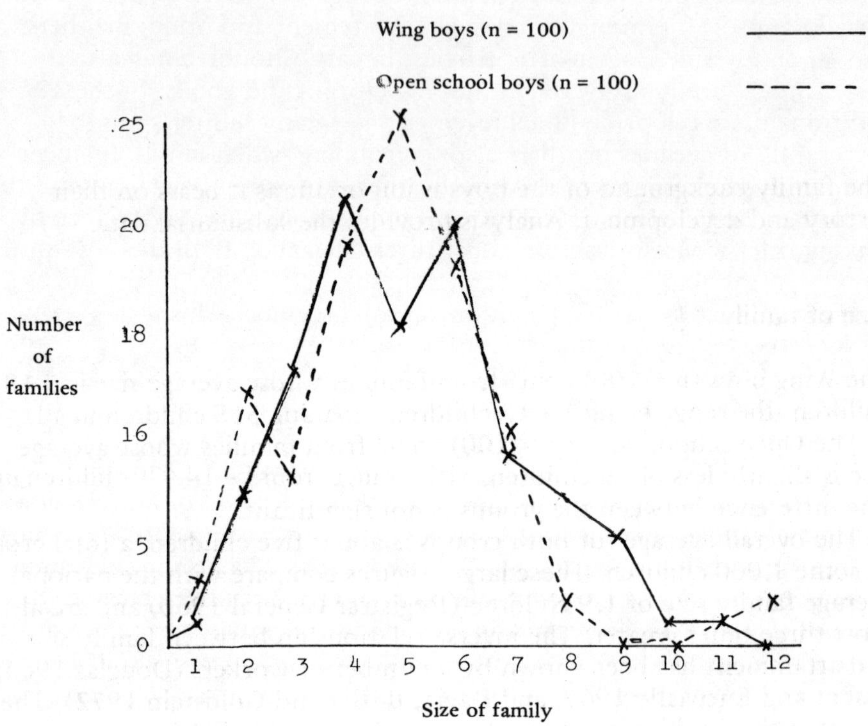

Figure 3.1 Size of families

Table 3.1

Size of families

Size of family	1	2	3	4	5	6	7	8	9	10	11	12	13	14
Wing boys (n = 100)	1	7	13	21	15	20	9	7	5	1	1	0	0	0
Open school boys (n = 100)	3	12	8	19	25	18	10	2	0	0	1	2	0	0

't' = 1.18, df = 198, $p > 0.10$ (not significant)

windows or over walls, effecting entry and opening doors from the inside for the others. For urban boys in areas of high delinquency this provides socially approved (among themselves) excitement and pride. Brothers also go on joy rides, often after parties, in cars. Shopbreaking also is sometimes a family affair to get money, clothes and goods. In these expeditions there is a pride of achievement, as in any hunter's mind, if successful. Sometimes brothers also 'go robbing' when family finances are low. In short, brothers draw each other into group behaviour and the thrill attendant. Becker (1963) wrote 'social groups create deviance by making rules whose infraction constitutes deviance'. If all the boys in the family 'go robbing' it is a social and cohesive activity for them, and to refuse would cause isolation and unfraternal feelings. This, however, does not hold between boys and parents.

Delinquent parents

The generation gap between boys and parents does not allow such comity in deviancy which is almost exclusively an adolescent activity. 'You don't go screwing (thieving) with your Da!' Few males over twenty continue such offences, for work, wives, children and responsibility change their ways of thought. They often stop 'getting into trouble', chaperoned by their own 'social worker', their wife, who has strong views about her husband risking prison or fines and being left alone while he is 'away with the boys' or 'inside'. Few develop into professional thieves as adults, and these are life's incompetents who eventually drift down skid row (Trasler 1962 and 1970) into recidivist custody. Most delinquent young men, as they grow up, settle down, marry and try to be good parents, protective of their offspring and quietly forget their adolescent deviance, except perhaps for the occasional jovial reference.

Enquiry, therefore, as to criminality in parents would be delicate and difficult and is generally inappropriate in psychological interviews. Boys can be defensive of family honour, of their father's and especially of the mother, who is nearly always protected no matter what her actions may be.

Considerable information on families, however, is contained in the social enquiry reports prepared for the Hearings or the Courts, but this is not exhaustive, for as time passes family data get sedimented into oblivion, forgotten deliberately, or merely not mentioned as being irrelevant when the family is being interviewed by the social worker.

The level of criminal history discovered in parents was low in both groups. Only two fathers were in prison at the time of the study, one for wife murder, and another for housebreaking. A third father had committed suicide in prison after being convicted for incest with his daughter.

Two boys reported that their fathers had 'done time' in the past. But otherwise the fathers (or father figures) living with the families are gainfully employed save those handicapped by illness or work injury. The general picture is of Social Class III (skilled manual) of good reputations. (Chapter 5 discusses this further.)

Some fathers (35 in the Wing and 36 in the Open school) have disappeared, and little is known; and it is probable that some fathers have themselves been in approved school, Borstal, or prison in the past but information obtained was too unreliable, being anecdotal, to be used as hard data. The Rushforth research (1978) on a similar population found a 10 per cent level of fathers with criminal records—a figure the present writer feels is also likely to relate to the fathers of the boys in the present study. There is not, however, evidence in the boys' files to substantiate this.

Birth rank in family

Adler held the view that birth position in the family affects the child's personality. It seemed of interest to pursue this idea in this study. Figure 3.2 and Table 3.2 indicate that both groups are very similar. The mode is for the third child in both groups, irrespective of family size, but more Wing boys are first-born than those in the Open school, i.e. 25 Wing boys as against 18 in the Open school. However, this difference is not significant ($x^2 = 1.4516$, df = 1, $p > 0.10$).

Figure 3.2 shows how closely the two groups resemble each other. Thus any influence birth rank may have is equally distributed among both groups of boys and so no inferences can be drawn, save that to be a third child may be a risky position.

Family data

Much social theory relates to the family situation of children. Empirical enquiry concerning each individual in this study in a variety of categories is therefore undertaken. Table 3.3 gives a broad outline, which will be expanded later in the discussion.

It is important to observe that the bird's eye view shown in Table 3.3 of families actually covers 400 people, the fathers and mothers of the 200 boys in this study, and it may be rendered as in Table 3.4 in terms of individuals, not families. When it is remembered that these 400 people have 1,000 children between them, we are considering a group of some 1,400 souls. The turbulence of the life patterns of each individual and the vicissitudes attendant are germane to the boys in our study. When the 'lost' fathers and mothers are also counted the figure is still higher.

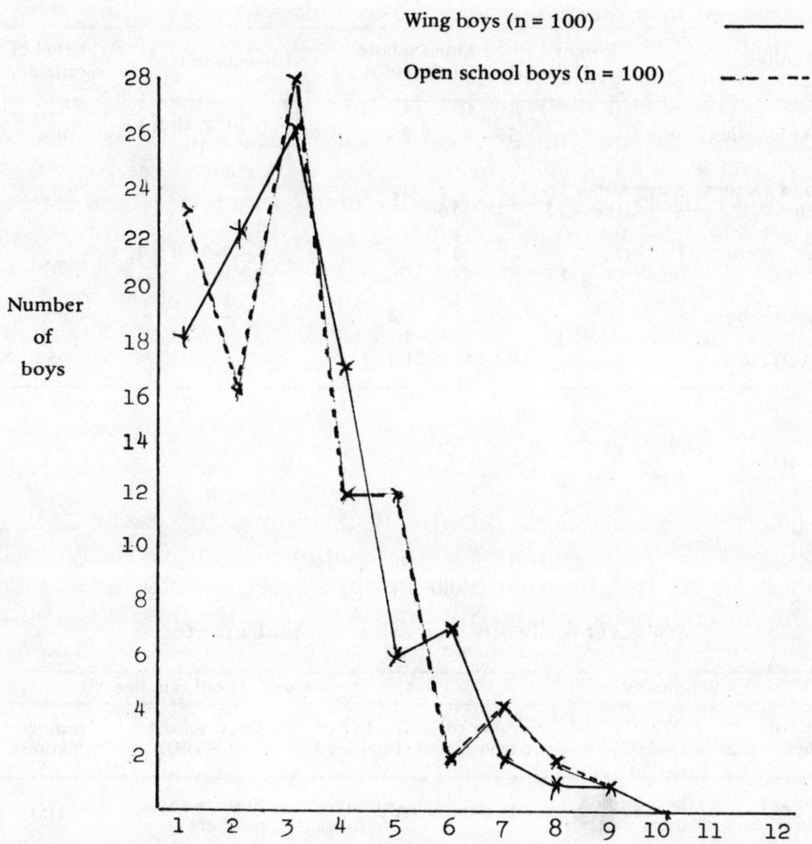

Figure 3.2 Birth rank in family

Table 3.2

Birth rank in family

Birth rank	1	2	3	4	5	6	7	8	9	10	11	12
Wing boys (n = 100)	18	22	26	17	6	7	2	1	1	0	0	0
Open school boys (n = 100)	23	16	28	12	12	2	4	2	1	0	0	0

By inspection it is clear there is no significant difference in these distributions

Table 3.3

Analysis of family data

Families		Wing (n = 100)		Open school (n = 100)		Chi-square test	Level of significance
1 Intact families			55		50	$x^2 = 0.5012$, df = 1, $p > 0.10$	n.s.
2 Second partner families	Stepmother Stepfather	6 15	21	5 16	21	–	n.s.
3 Single parent families	Fathers Mothers	6 17	23	10 17	27	$x^2 = 0.4266$, df = 1, $p > 0.10$	n.s.
4 Parentless boys			1		2	–	n.s
TOTAL			100		100	–	–

Table 3.4

Analysis of family data expressed as individual parents

Wing families				Open school families		
	Number of families	Wing (n = 100)	Number of parents	Number of families	Open school (n = 100)	Number of parents
1	55 Intact families	Fathers and mothers	110	50 Intact families	Fathers and mothers	100
2	21 Second partner families	6 fathers remarry = 12 15 mothers remarry = 30	42	21 Second partner families	5 fathers remarry = 10 16 mothers remarry = 32	42
3	23 Single parents	6 fathers lost 6 wives = 12 17 mothers lost 17 men = 34	46	27 Single parents	10 fathers lost 10 wives = 20 17 mothers lost 17 men = 34	54
4	1 Orphan	2 lost parents	2	2 Orphans	4 lost parents	4
	100		200	100		200

1 *Intact families*

Inspection of Tables 3.3 and 3.4 reveals that nearly half the parents in both groups live together as intact nuclear families, 55 families in the Wing group and 50 families in the Open school group. This difference is not significant statistically. Thus the family picture for half the cohort of both groups appears favourable, at first sight, though less so for the other half.

2 *Second partner families*

It will be seen from Table 3.3 that 21 boys in each group have parents whose first marriages had failed or ended by death and had formed a second stable union, either by remarriage or by cohabitation. That the number of reunions is the same is surprising; but even more surprising is the fact that almost the same number of mothers and fathers did re-marry, 15 and 16 mothers and 6 and 5 fathers in the Wing and Open school groups respectively. Thus three times as many stepfathers are represented as stepmothers, eleven stepmothers as contrasted with 31 stepfathers overall ($x^2 = 10.386$, df = 1, $p < 0.001$). Perhaps women form new alliances more frequently than men, for companionship, and for help in raising their children. An alternative explanation of these figures is that stepfathers in the cohort cause alienation of the boy and his subsequent delinquency more frequently than do stepmothers. Certainly boys in the study express hostility in plenty, when interviewed, concerning these replacement fathers. For the teenage boy sexual jealousy of the mother may well play a part in this stepfather–boy situation, each jealous of the other.

3 *Single parents*

Single parents are numbered overall 23 in the Wing and 27 in the Open school—a difference not significant statistically. 17 mothers in both groups were rearing their children alone, and nobly, and perhaps unexpectedly in a Scottish matriarchal society, six fathers in the Wing and ten fathers in the Open school. This difference is not significant statistically ($x^2 = 1.0869$, df = 1, $p > 0.10$).

4 *Parentless boys*

In the two groups three boys had no families, one in the Wing and two in the Open school.

Summary. Thus in aggregate, nearly three-quarters of the families contain a male and female figure, either natural parents or step-parents, 76 in the Wing and 71 in the Open school (see Table 3.3). This difference is not statistically significant.

Parental loss

It is clear from Table 3.5 that no significant difference in regard to lost parents obtains between the Wing boys and the Open school boys. Both are equally unfortunate.

It also appears that, except in the families with two natural parents, it is mainly the mother who is the anchor figure for the boy remaining in her care despite domestic vicissitudes.

Table 3.5

Families who have lost father, mother or both

	Wing (n = 100)	Open school (n = 100)	Chi-square test	Level of significance
Mother lost	12	15	$x^2 = 0.3853$, df = 1, $p > 0.10$	n.s.
Father lost	32	33	–	–
Both lost	1	2	–	–
Total non-intact families	45	50	$x^2 = 0.512$, df = 1, p 0.10	n.s.
Intact families	55	50	$x^2 = 0.5012$, df = 1, $p > 0.10$	n.s.
TOTAL	100	100	–	–

Mother loss versus father loss

For a comparison of mothers' and fathers' tenacity to their children when the nuclear family is not intact see Table 3.6.

Table 3.6

Mother loss compared to father loss

	Mothers lost	Fathers lost	Chi-square test	Level of significance
Wing	13	33	$x^2 = 11.29$, df = 1, $0.01 > p > 0.001$	0.01
Open school	17	35	$x^2 = 4.91$, df = 1, $0.02 > p > 0.01$	0.05
TOTAL including orphans	30	68	$x^2 = 9.19$, df = 1, $p > 0.01$	0.01

It is abundantly clear that fathers vanish from the boys' lives much more than mothers do. Of the 45 non-intact families in the Wing, 33 fathers have been lost but only 13 mothers (see Tables 3.5 and 3.6). In the Open school of the 50 unintact families (50 are intact), 35 fathers have disappeared from the boys' lives and only 7 mothers. The maternal bonds are significantly stronger. Fathers inseminate, mothers carry the child, and look after it; the metaphorical umbilical cord does not wither. Mothers who disappear do so after infancy is past. Age of parental loss will be discussed fully later in this chapter (see Tables 3.14, 3.15 and 3.18).

Again there is no significant difference between the two groups of boys in these dimensions.

Summary of family analysis

The family situation of the boys in the Wing and the Open school is remarkably similar as regards parental patterns of behaviour. Intact families are not significantly different in number. Parents who form second partnerships, both fathers and mothers, are identical in numbers, with stepfathers featuring significantly more often than stepmothers in both groups. Possible explanations may be that more women than men form second marriages, or that more breakdowns occur in relationships between boys and stepfathers due to jealousies over the mother.

Numbers of single parent mothers are the same in both groups, i.e. 17. Single parent fathers are more frequent in the Open school group, ten as opposed to six, but the difference is not significant.

Boys in both groups have lost almost the same number of mothers and fathers but mothers are significantly more permanent than fathers for boys with non-intact nuclear families in both groups (see Table 3.6).

The number of parentless boys is low and almost the same: one in the Wing, two in the Open school.

In short, the parallel numbers of intact families, second unions, single parents and orphans are not only not significantly different statistically but also almost identical in actual numbers.

It is therefore clear that in family dynamics the parental situation of both groups shows no significant differences. Compared, however, to a normal population, parental loss is high in both groups. In aggregate for the total cohort of 200 families, 27 have lost a mother and 65 have lost a father; three are without either (see Tables 3.5 and 3.6). 95 families from the total 200 are impaired (see Table 3.3).

Employment of parents

Analysis of the four groups of families (see Table 3.3) now follows in terms of employment.

Intact families

The 'intact' families are those whose father and mother live together in the same house with their children in the nuclear group. Of these there were 55 in the Wing and 50 in the Open school. Their family patterns of employment, handicap and unemployment are shown in Table 3.7 and in Figure 3.3.

Table 3.7

Employment of parents; intact families

	Wing (n = 110 parents, fathers and mothers)	Open school (n = 100 parents, fathers and mothers)	Chi-square test	Level of significance
(a) Employed parents				
Fathers	29	36	$x^2 = 1.1168$, df = 1, $p > 0.10$	n.s.
Mothers	21	29	$x^2 = 1.7066$, df = 1, $p > 0.10$	n.s.
(b) Handicapped parents				
Fathers	23	12	$x^2 = 4.1905$, df = 1, $0.05 > p > 0.01$	0.05
Mothers	0	1		
(c) Housekeeping parents				
Fathers	0	0		
Mothers	34	20	$x^2 = 4.972$, df = 1, $0.05 > p > 0.01$	0.05
(d) Unemployed parents				
Fathers	3	2		
Mothers	–	–		
TOTAL of parents	110	100		

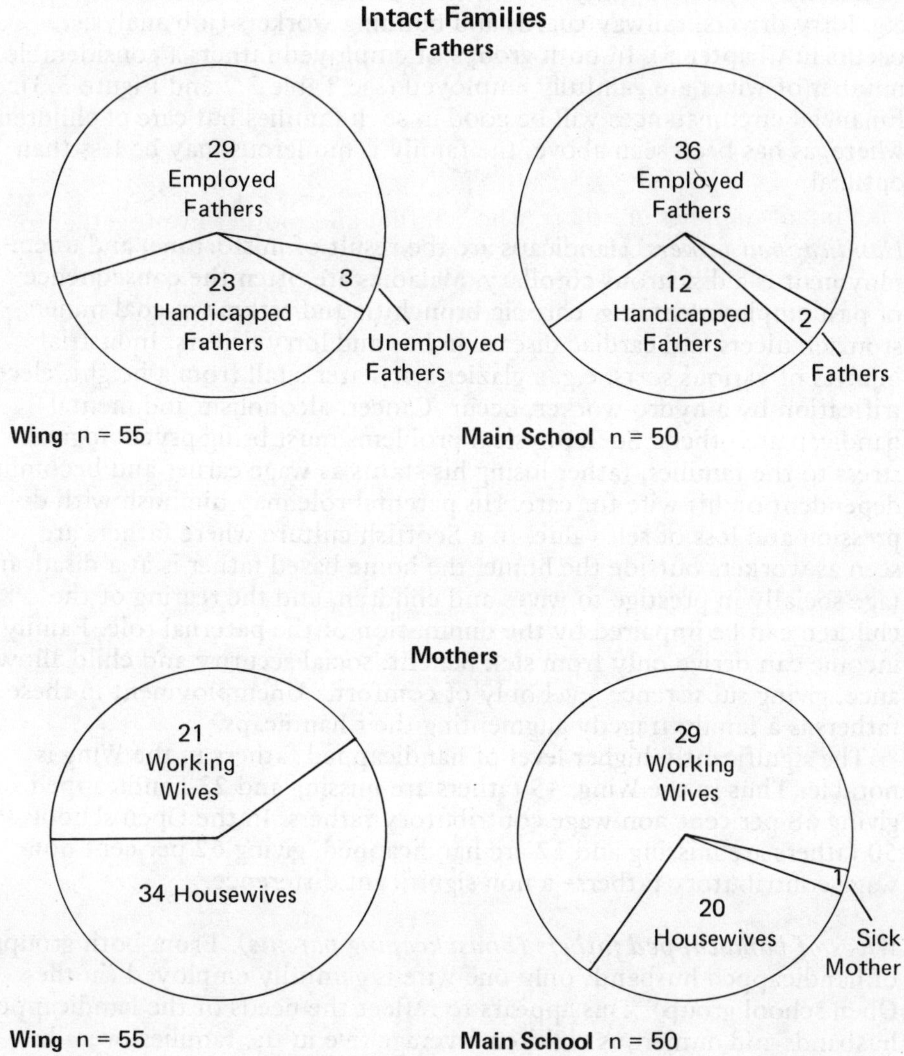

Figure 3.3 Employment of parents; intact families

A significantly larger number of fathers in the Wing are handicapped as compared to the Open school fathers.

The unemployment level is not significantly different.

Many more mothers are housewives in the Wing than in the Open school group, probably relating to the higher number of handicapped husbands there.

Physically fit fathers. Only few of the jobs necessitate work absence, e.g. lorry drivers, railway guards and building workers (job analysis occurs in Chapter 5). In both groups of employed fathers a considerable number of wives are gainfully employed (see Table 3.7 and Figure 3.3). Financial circumstances will be good in such families but care of children where, as has been seen above, the family is numerous may be less than optimal.

Handicapped fathers. Handicaps are the result of misfortune, and unemployment is a disastrous corollary. Maladies are often the consequence of past employment, e.g. chronic bronchitis and asthma in coal miners, stomach ulcers and cardiac disease in bus and lorry drivers. Industrial injuries of various sorts, e.g. a glazier's or slater's fall from a height, electrification by a hydro worker, occur. Cancer, alcoholism and mental handicap are others. Such physical problems must bring psychological stress to the families, father losing his status as wage earner and becoming dependent on his wife for care. His parental role may diminish with depression and loss of self value. In a Scottish culture where fathers are seen as workers outside the home, the home based father is at a disadvantage socially in prestige to wives and children, and the rearing of the children can be impaired by the diminution of the paternal role. Family income can derive only from sick benefit, social security and child allowance, giving subsistence level only of comfort. Unemployment in these fathers is a family tragedy augmenting their handicaps.

The significantly higher level of handicapped fathers in the Wing is notable. Thus in the Wing, 45 fathers are missing and 23 handicapped giving 68 per cent non-wage contributory fathers. In the Open school 50 fathers are missing and 12 are handicapped, giving 62 per cent non-wage contributory fathers—a non-significant difference.

Wives of handicapped fathers (housekeeping parents). From both groups of handicapped husbands only one wife is gainfully employed (in the Open school group). This appears to reflect the needs of the handicapped husbands and numerous children (average five in the families overall, see Table 3.1) for constant attendance. The income of the family, with no wage earner, must be low.

Housekeeping parents. The situation mirrors the higher numbers of handicapped fathers.

Unemployed fathers. These figures are perhaps surprising in a Scottish population where unemployment is at a high level overall. Moreover, it is possible that the unemployment of these few physically fit fathers is only seasonal.

Summary

Employment is high for the physically fit fathers; and below the national average for unemployment.

Employment for mothers in both groups of working fathers is not significantly different, reflecting the growing place of women in the employment market. Nevertheless, with large families, averaging five children in each, with a range from 1 to 14, child care may not be high.

The important difference between the groups is in the significantly higher number of handicapped and consequently unemployed fathers. In the Scottish matriarchal society this will involve not only financial but social and psychological disadvantage—income deriving solely from social benefit.

A further similarity between the groups is that the wives of the handicapped fathers are not gainfully employed, save one in the Open school. Money will be scarce for all such families. Significantly more Wing mothers are therefore non-wage earning as more Wing fathers are handicapped.

In short, except for the significantly higher number of handicapped fathers and housewife mothers, the situation of the intact families is the same in the Wing as in the Open school.

Even for the intact nuclear family the picture on examination is not entirely rosy. Families are large and both parents are working when the father is physically fit. In the families where fathers are handicapped, mothers do not work. Twice the number of Wing fathers are handicapped as the Open school fathers, 23 per cent of the Wing group as opposed to 12 per cent of the Open school group. This brings them both social and financial disadvantage.

Families in both groups have a high level of non-wage earning natural fathers, because of broken families and because of handicapped fathers. Figures are 68 per cent non-wage contributory natural fathers in the Wing and 62 per cent non-wage contributory natural fathers in the Open school—this difference is not significant statistically ($x^2 = 0.28$, df = 1, $p > 0.10$). Such a high level of disadvantage in both groups is important to note.

Second partner families

When parents separate or divorce or when one partner dies, further liaisons occur leading to remarriage or cohabitation and both in this study are counted as second partners. From the view of the children involved a new member of the household, replacing the lost partner, brings change and stress. This may lead to accommodation and to amelioration of the family patterns. The National Childrens' Bureau study (Davie et al 1972) found a nationally high level of success in such second partnerships. For the particular boys in this study this does not appear to occur, perhaps because of attitudes inside the family after the new liaison, and perhaps (and probably also) because of previous stresses while the primary parental figures were still in action in the family dynamics. Conditions obtaining in early childhood need great skills to reverse (Clarke and Clarke 1976). The cases here discussed are the failures for the children of the second partner situation.

Table 3.4 shows that in the Wing 21 parents remarried, 6 fathers and 15 mothers, and the same number remarried in the Open school but here there were 5 fathers and 16 mothers. The employment situation for both partners is examined in Table 3.8. The parallel is close for both groups and there are again no significant differences.

Table 3.8

Second partner families, employment, handicap and unemployment

Wing (n = 21)				Open school (n = 21)	
Fathers (n = 6) who remarry		Stepmothers (n = 6)		Fathers (n = 5) who remarry	Stepmothers (n = 5)
Employed	6	Wage-earning stepmother	1	4	3
Unemployed	0		0	1	0
Housewives	–		5	–	2
TOTALS	6		6	5	5
Mothers (n = 15) who remarry		Stepfathers (n = 15)		Mothers (n = 16) who remarry	Stepfathers (n = 16)
Employed	3		14	10	15
Handicapped unemployed	0		1	0	1 *
Housewives	12		–	6	–
TOTALS	15		15	16	16

* One stepfather in prison

In Table 3.8 parallels are self-evident in the total of figures and no significant differences appear between the groups.

It is interesting, as has been discussed above, that more stepfathers than stepmothers occur in both groups.

The majority of the women have married men as second husbands who are in work, with the exception of one in the Wing group who is agoraphobic and alcoholic, and one in the Open school group who is in prison.

The fathers in the Wing group have mainly housewife second partners. However, in the Open school group three out of the five new wives are wage-earning workers.

More mothers have remained as caring parents than have fathers (or possibly remarrying fathers do not have boys who get into trouble and so are absent from our study).

Summary

Second partner marriages appear prosperous for the parents though sons are deviant.

There is no difference in the family patterns between the groups.

One parent families

Families may lose one or other parent by death, desertion or divorce and do not remarry. Some mothers have never had a husband and bring up their illegitimate offspring on their own or with the help of the extended family. Fathers who try to care for their children as single parents are particularly vulnerable when the children are young and eldest daughters receive the heaviest burden thereby. Boys, in our study, admit to resisting helping with family chores, escaping to the peer group life of the streets and to the risk of being sucked into delinquency.

Table 3.9

Single parent fathers and employment

Fathers	Wing (n = 6)	Open school (n = 10)	Chi-square test	Level of significance
Employed	5	8	$x^2 = 0.7404$, df = 1, $p > 0.10$	n.s.
In prison	1*	0	–	–
Unemployed gainfully	0	2 (Housekeepers)	–	–
TOTALS	6	10	$x^2 = 1.0868$, df = 1, $p > 0.10$	n.s.

*The father in prison in the Wing was guilty of wife murder. He is a father of middle class status, once owner of a garage. His son, when in the Wing, visited him regularly and letters were frequently exchanged. Parole was hoped for soon after his son's own release. (Unhappily the boy went to Borstal within weeks of release from the Wing.)

Table 3.9 shows the picture for the single parent fathers. Of the two 'unemployed' fathers in the Open school group, both were 'housekeepers'. One had five young children to care for and remained at home to avoid their going into care. The other father was a plasterer's labourer, living in an area of low employment 'going each week to the employment office without getting anything', in his son's defensive words. He cared for his six children for some years after his wife's death before the family was taken into care through the intervention of the RSPCC.

Table 3.10

Cause of loss of mother in one parent families

	Wing (n = 6)	Open school (n = 10)	Chi-square test	Level of significance
Divorce or separation	1	1	–	–
Death (natural)	3	2	–	–
Murdered (by father)	1*	0	–	–
Deserted	1	7	–	–
TOTAL	6	10	$x^2 = 1.0892$, df = 1 $p > 0.10$	n.s.

*See Table 3.9

Summary

Overall there are no significant differences between the two groups as regards single parent fathers.

Single parent mothers

In the same extraordinary way the number of single mothers in both groups is identical. Slightly more mothers are gainfully employed in the Open school group and more are housewives in the Wing group (see Table 3.11). The differences between the groups is not significant statistically.

Table 3.11

Single parent mothers and employment

Wing		Open school		Chi-square test	Level of significance
Mothers (n = 17)		Mothers (n = 17)		–	n.s.
Employed	4	Employed	7	$x^2 = 0.8658$, df = 1, $p > 0.10$	n.s.
Housewives	13	Housewives	10	$x^2 = 0.44215$, df = 1, $p > 0.10$	n.s.
TOTALS	17		17	–	–

Table 3.12

Cause of loss of father in one parent families

Cause	Wing (n = 17)	Open school (n = 17)	Level of significance
Divorce or separation	7	5	–
Desertion	4	3	–
Death (natural)	4	1	–
Illegitimacy	1	5	–
Car accident	1	0	–
Murdered	0	1*	–
Drowned at sea	0	1	–
Suicide in prison	0	1†	–
TOTAL	17	17	n.s.

*This case was of a father mugged in a street alley in Glasgow, robbed of his pay packet and murdered.

†This case was of a father imprisoned for 'lewd and libidinous practices' to his daughters who hanged himself in his cell. It may be supposed that opinion in the prison was unfavourable towards him.

It is inevitably easier in our culture for mothers to rear children as single parents than for fathers. Society is more sympathetic and understanding. Yet for both the difficulties are high, bringing loss of confidence, depression, poverty and fatigue; it is also difficult to be gainfully employed and to care for young children.

Single parent mothers are more numerous than single parent fathers in both groups. Illegitimate children fall in their care, five of whom are in the Open school and one in the Wing.

In all, single parent families, both fathers and mothers, comprise 23 families from the Wing (n = 100) and 27 families from the Open school (n = 100) (see Tables 3.3 and 3.13). This is nearly a quarter of both cohorts. The level of deprivation in this group must obviously be high.

Table 3.13

Single parent families, fathers and mothers

	Wing (n = 100)	Open school (n = 100)	Chi-square test	Level of significance
Single fathers	6	10	$x^2 = 1.10849$, df = 1, $p > 0.10$	n.s.
Single mothers	17	17	–	n.s.
Total of single parents	23	27	$x^2 = 0.43$, df = 1, $p > 0.10$	n.s.

Boys in the Wing and the Open school have equal numbers of single parent mothers and the small difference between the single parent fathers is not significant statistically. Thus the extraordinary parallel continues.

Combining the number of single parent boys in both the Wing and the Open school, we find 50 boys (see Table 3.13). Of these 34 have single parent mothers and 16 have single parent fathers. In all 25 per cent of the total group of boys have single parent families and, as has been remarked earlier, mothers cling to the boys more than fathers.

Parentless boys

One boy in the Wing, illegitimate and with four siblings, was orphaned when his mother took an overdose.

Two boys in the Open school, one a member of six children deserted by both parents, and another illegitimate and abandoned, are without families. The numbers are too small for any analysis.

Home bases

Boys in residential institutions have great need of a home base for leave and holidays. Otherwise they are an embarrassment to the institution and dispirited in themselves. Happily nearly all the boys, except the three boys without any family brought up in a multiplicity of institutions, have a home base and family of sorts to whom they turn, one way or another, of whatever kind. They want to be home. With an average of four siblings (a range from 1 to 14 children in the families) the homes will be lively and friendly and belonging to them as private individuals, not as members of an institution. They 'belong' at home.

Colin (15+), whose psychological report now follows, is one of these parentless and homeless boys.

Psychological testing

Vernon graded word reading test:	reading age 9 years
Wechsler intelligence scale for children (sub-test 3)	arithmetic test age: 9 years
Wechsler intelligence scale for children	average ability handwriting: poor

Psychological report

Colin is a boy who presents a picture of pathos. His mother died on 30 March 1976 after having been in a coma for about three months. The social enquiry report suggests that the coma was engendered by an overdose. His mother had five illegitimate children of whom Colin was the only boy. It appears that the family live in an area of high delinquency but nevertheless the family had good standards, avoiding petty crime, but attracting the attention of the social work department on account of school avoidance. It is possible that their illegitimacy may have made them distressed because of teasing at school and thus made school unhappy for them.

After the death of the mother the older girls looked after the children until aunts and other members of the extended family took over this duty. An older girl is shortly going to Kuwait to be married to a Kuwaiti engineer.

Colin is a boy with very pleasant manners, but a diffident and sad demeanour. He has been in homes nearly all his life sporadically on account of school refusal. At the age of seven he was placed in a national childrens' home. He said that he was very happy there and the first smile appeared on his face during the interview when he talked of this time. Eventually he left but his school refusal continued together with petty delinquency. His next placement was in another childrens' home. Initially he did well and at a review Hearing there were commending remarks on his progress; however as he grew older he began to abscond from the home and to fail to return from home visits. The social enquiry report notes that the boy spent long periods at home with his mother doing household chores. It also notes that Colin tended to be bullied by his classmates and that he did not enjoy the normal games small boys play. His concentration on his mother's care is diagnostic of his need for affection. His persistent absconding from the home brought him into considerable disfavour with the authorities.

After return to his mother a social work report described Colin as watching television until late at night and then wandering the streets in such a manner that the mother became extremely worried and had no idea as to what he was doing. He also ceased to co-operate with the social worker, evading contact with her by escaping through windows or by vanishing in some other fashion.

Throughout the interview Colin maintained his courteous mannerly behaviour, occasionally smiling but talking seriously of himself and his problems with a discretion which was marked. He expressed obvious grief for his mother and it is clear that his period of mourning is still holding.

His main anxiety was that his aunt, who has offered him hospitality during his leaves, should be reminded to return the form giving consent to accept him. He said that his aunt was very forgetful and might easily fail to return the form although he knew that she was fond of him and that he was very welcome in her home. He also asked for the address of his home social worker so that he could write to him and thus maintain a link with his home environment. He said that he was also writing consistently to his sisters and that they were responding and sending him parcels.

The pathos this boy presents and the lack of privilege he is experiencing in his life, with the death of his mother also, is marked.

Recommendation

Further contact with Colin as may be practicable.

Some boys, less fortunate than Colin, have no parents and have no relatives who will take them for holidays and leave weekends. They must therefore go to hostels, assessment centres or childrens' homes, lodgings often less acceptable than their List D school where, at least, they know where they are.

Boys' ages at loss of parents

It appears from Figure 3.4 and Table.3.14 that most Wing boys lost parents between the ages of six and twelve, later in maturity than the Open school boys. The Open school boys' losses are spread more widely through the age groups, with more in early childhood. The higher parent (father) loss at infancy reflects the illegitimacy rate, five in the Open school, one in the Wing.

Statistical analysis by 't' test, however, shows no significant difference between the groups. Chance would account for the apparent differences in ages throughout.

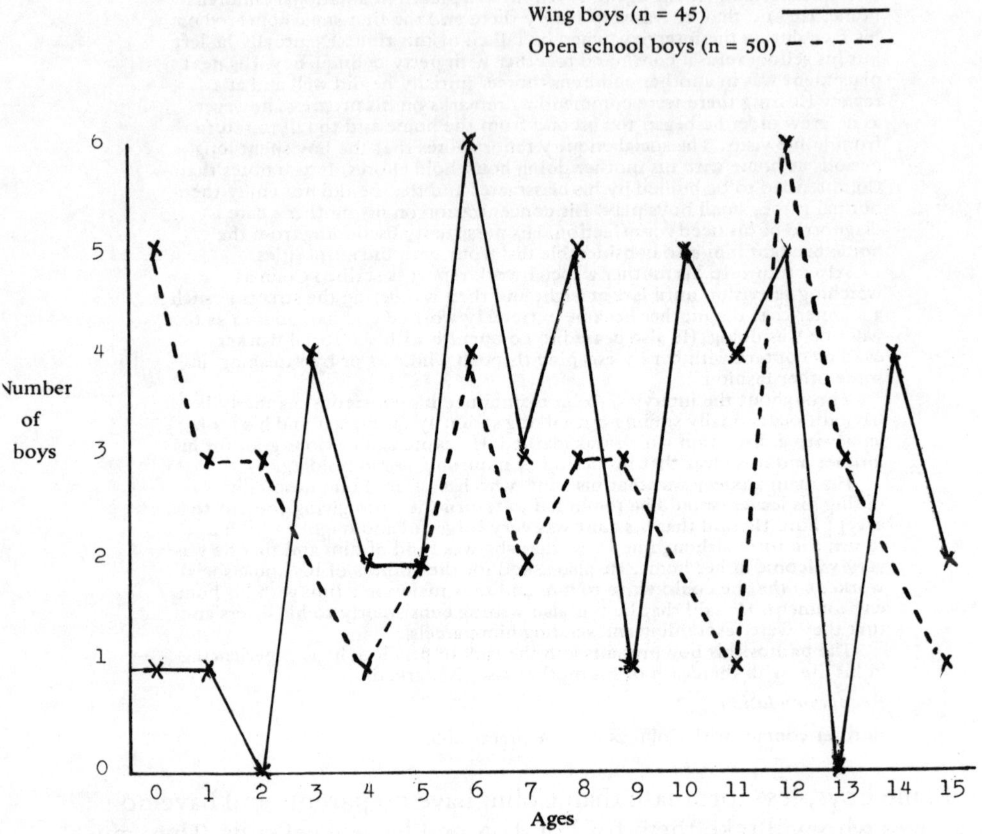

Figure 3.4 Boys' ages at loss of parents

Table 3.14

Boys' ages at loss of parents

Age at loss	0	1	2	3	4	5	6	7	8	9	10	11	12	13	14	15
Wing (n = 45)	1	1	0	4	2	2	6	3	5	1	5	4	5	0	4	2
Open school (n = 50)	5	3	3	4	1	2	4	2	3	3	5	1	6	3	4	1

't' = 1.157, $p > 0.20$ when $df = 93$ (no statistical difference)

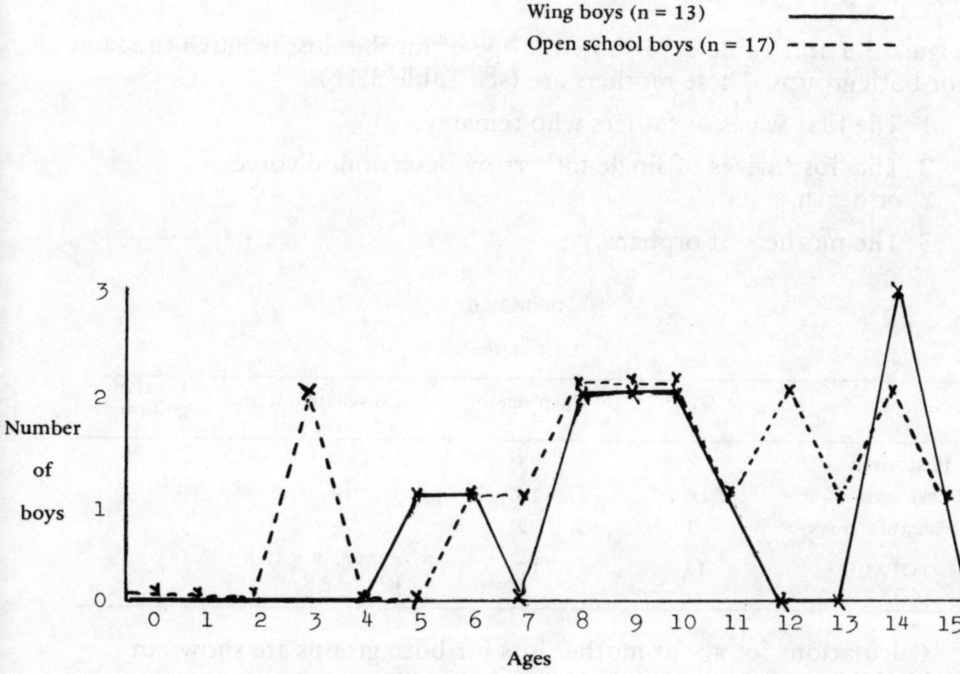

Figure 3.5 Boys' ages at loss of mother

Table 3.15

Boys' ages at loss of mother

Age at loss	0	1	2	3	4	5	6	7	8	9	10	11	12	13	14	15
Wing (n = 13)	0	0	0	0	0	1	1	0	2	2	2	1	0	0	3	1
Open school (n = 17)	0	0	0	2	0	0	1	1	2	2	2	1	2	1	2	1

't' = 0.45, df = 28, p > 0.10 (no significant difference)

Age of boys at loss of mother

Figure 3.5 and Table 3.15 show the age of mother loss is much the same for both groups. These mothers are (see Table 3.16):

1 The first wives of fathers who remarry.
2 The 'lost' wives of single fathers by desertion, divorce or death.
3 The mothers of orphans.

Table 3.16

Lost mothers

	Wing	Open school	Chi-square test	Level of significance
First wives	6	5	–	
Lost wives	6	10	–	
Parentless boys	1	2	–	
TOTAL	13	17	$x^2 = 0.63$, df = 1, $p > 0.10$	n.s.

Calculations for age at mother loss for both groups are shown in Table 3.17.

Table 3.17

Mean age at loss of mother

	Wing	Open school
Mean age (years)	10.23	9.65
Significant difference	3.10	3.47
TOTAL (lost mothers)	13	17

The difference is not significant ('t' = 0.45, df = 28, $p > 0.10$).

The hypothesis that disturbed children derive from maternal loss in early childhood does not appear to hold in either group. The Wing group loses its first mother at age five and the Open school group has two losses at age three but none at ages four and five. Bowlby (1953, 1959 and 1973) and Clarke and Clarke (1976) might argue that poor maternal care might be as harmful as loss of the mother in the group now studied.

Separation from mother in early childhood

It was not possible to obtain hard data on possible early separations, even

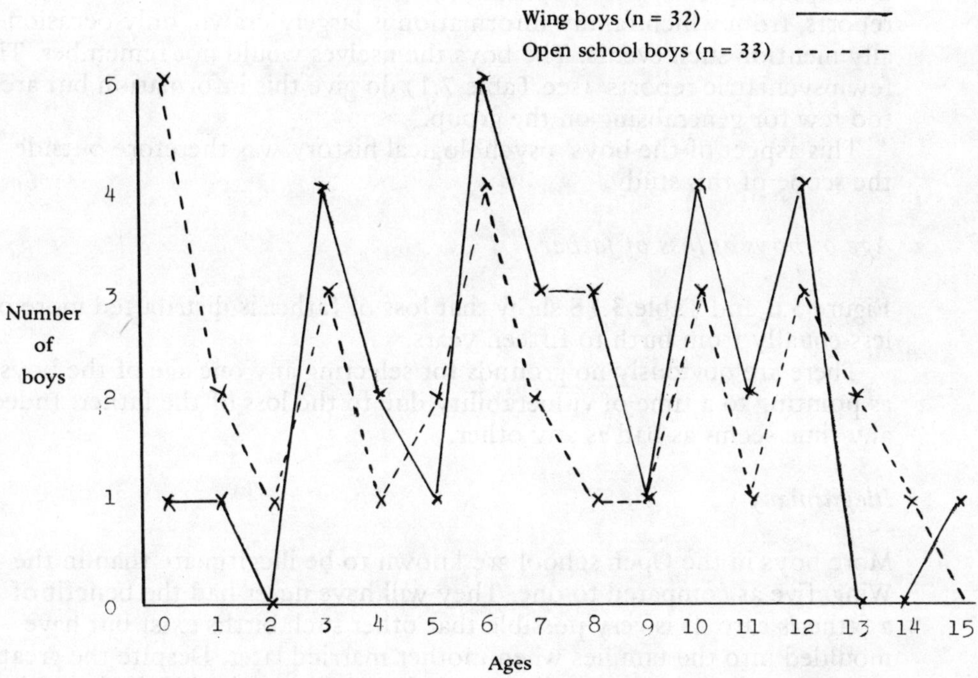

Figure 3.6 Boys' ages at loss of father

Table 3.18

Boys' ages at loss of father

Age at loss	0	1	2	3	4	5	6	7	8	9	10	11	12	13	14	15
Wing (n = 32)	1	1	0	4	2	1	5	3	3	1	4	2	4	0	0	1
Open school (n = 33)	5	2	1	3	1	2	4	2	1	1	3	1	3	2	2	0

Mean age of Wing boys' father loss = 7.34 years

Mean age of Open school boys' father loss = 6.45 years

't' = 0.86, df = 63, $p > 0.10$ (the mean difference in age of father loss is not significant)

if temporarily due to hospitalisation, from maternal care. Social enquiry reports, from which family information is largely drawn, only occasionally mention such events. The boys themselves would not remember. The few psychiatric reports (see Table 7.1) do give this information but are too few for generalising on the group.

This aspect of the boys' psychological history was therefore outside the scope of this study.

Age of boys at loss of father

Figure 3.6 and Table 3.18 show that loss of father is distributed more or less equally from birth to fifteen years.

There are obviously no grounds for selecting any one age of the boys as pointing to a time of vulnerability due to the loss of the father. Indeed any time seems as bad as any other.

Illegitimacy

More boys in the Open school are known to be illegitimate than in the Wing, five as compared to one. They will have never had the benefit of a father's care. It is very possible that other such births exist but have moulded into the families when mother married later. Despite the greater number of illegitimates in the Open school, the number of single mothers in both groups is nevertheless the same, i.e. 17.

Death of parents

15 parents have died, 9 in the Wing group and 6 in the Open school group (see Table 3.19). These are the partners whose spouses are now either single parents or have formed new unions or the parents of the orphans. No significant difference appears between the parent deaths of Wing or Open school boys. But 7½ per cent (15 : 200) of parental death is higher than the national average for parents of adolescent children.

Table 3.19

Death of parents

	Fathers	Mothers	Chi-square test	Level of significance
Wing	5	4	$x^2 = 0.1163$, df = 1, $p > 0.10$	n.s.
Open school	4	2	$x^2 = 0.6872$, df = 1, $p > 0.10$	n.s.
TOTAL	9	6	$x^2 = 0.649$, df = 1, $p > 0.10$	n.s.

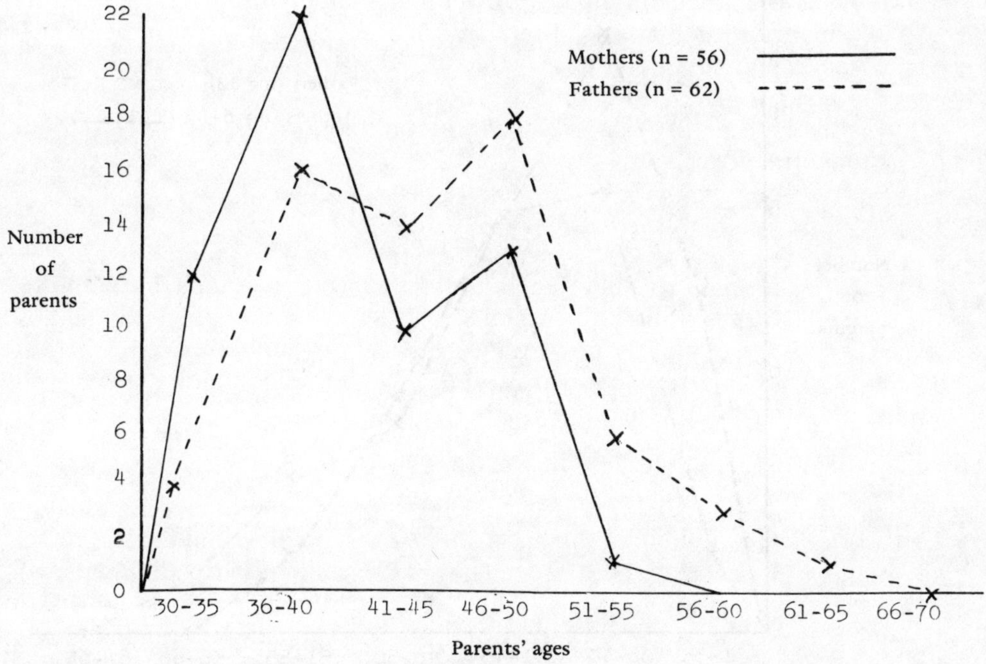

Figure 3.7 Age of Wing boys' natural parents

Table 3.20
Age of Wing boys' natural parents

Age	30-35	36-40	41-45	46-50	51-55	56-60	61-65	66-70
Mothers (n = 56)	12	22	10	13	1	0	0	0
Fathers (n = 62)	4	16	14	18	6	3	1	0

It is obvious that fathers are older than mothers; also 't' = 3.72, df = 116, p > 0.001 (significant difference)

Mothers' mean age = 40.33 years, sd = 5.49, n = 58
Fathers' mean age = 44.53 years, sd = 6.71, n = 62

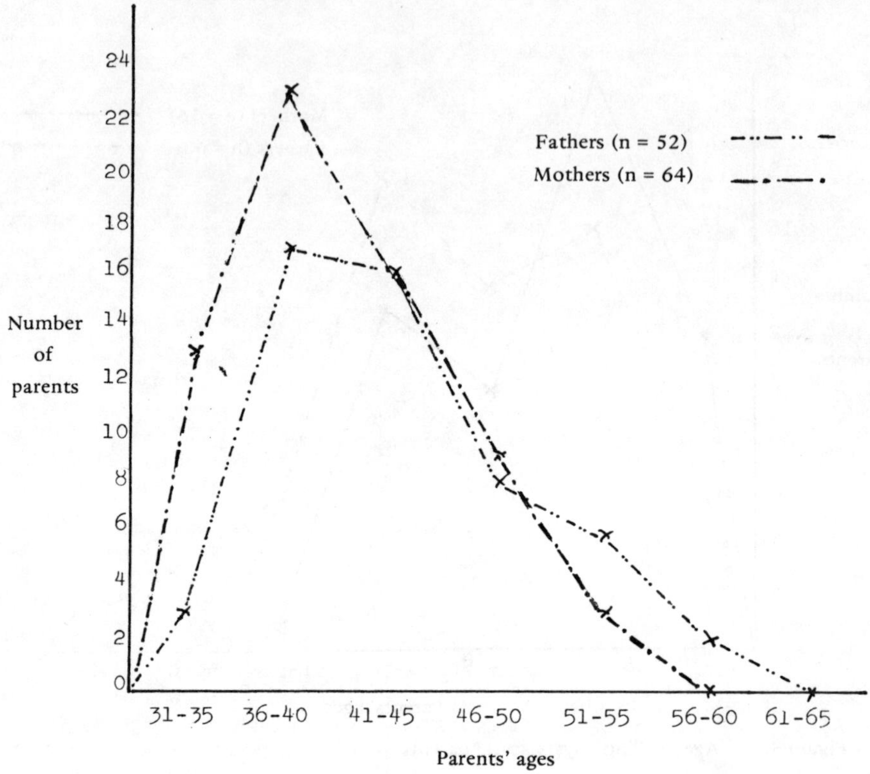

Figure 3.8 Age of Open school boys' natural parents

Table 3.21

Age of Open school boys' natural parents

Age	31-35	36-40	41-45	46-50	51-55	56-60	61-65
Fathers (n = 52)	3	17	16	8	6	2	0
Mothers (n = 64)	13	23	16	9	3	0	0

Fathers are significantly older than mothers ('t' = 2.66, df = 114, $0.01 > p > 0.001$)

Fathers' mean age = 43.29 years, sd = 6.15

Mothers' mean age = 34 years, sd = 5.54

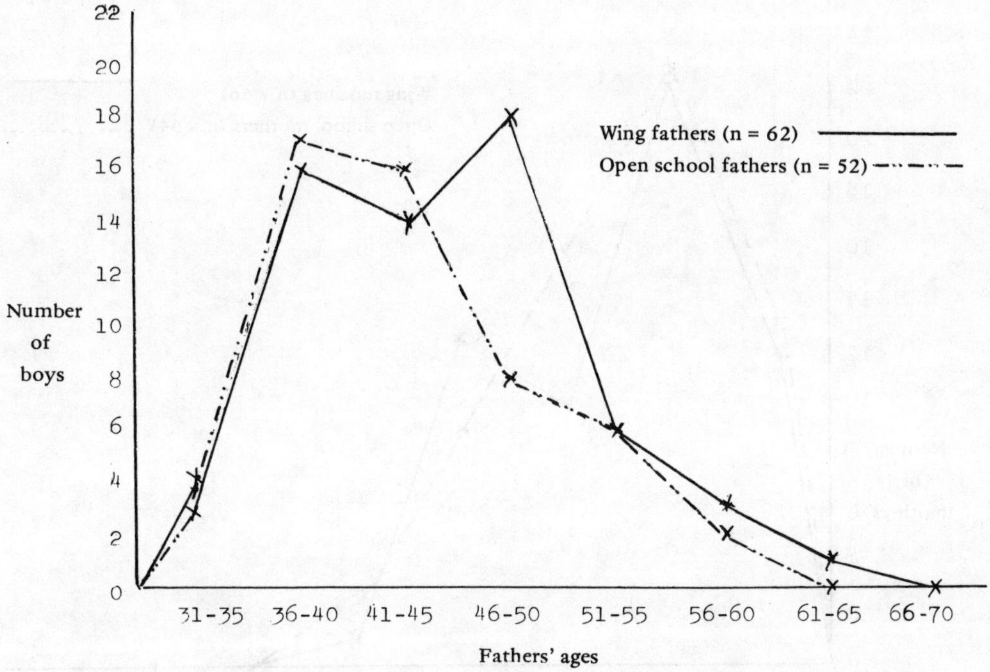

Figure 3.9 Fathers' ages in both groups compared

Table 3.22

Fathers' ages in both groups compared

Age	31-35	36-40	41-45	46-50	51-55	56-60	61-65	66-70
Wing (n = 62)	4	16	14	18	6	3	1	0
Open school (n = 52)	3	17	16	8	6	2	0	0

't' = 1.016, df = 112, p> 0.20 (no significant difference)

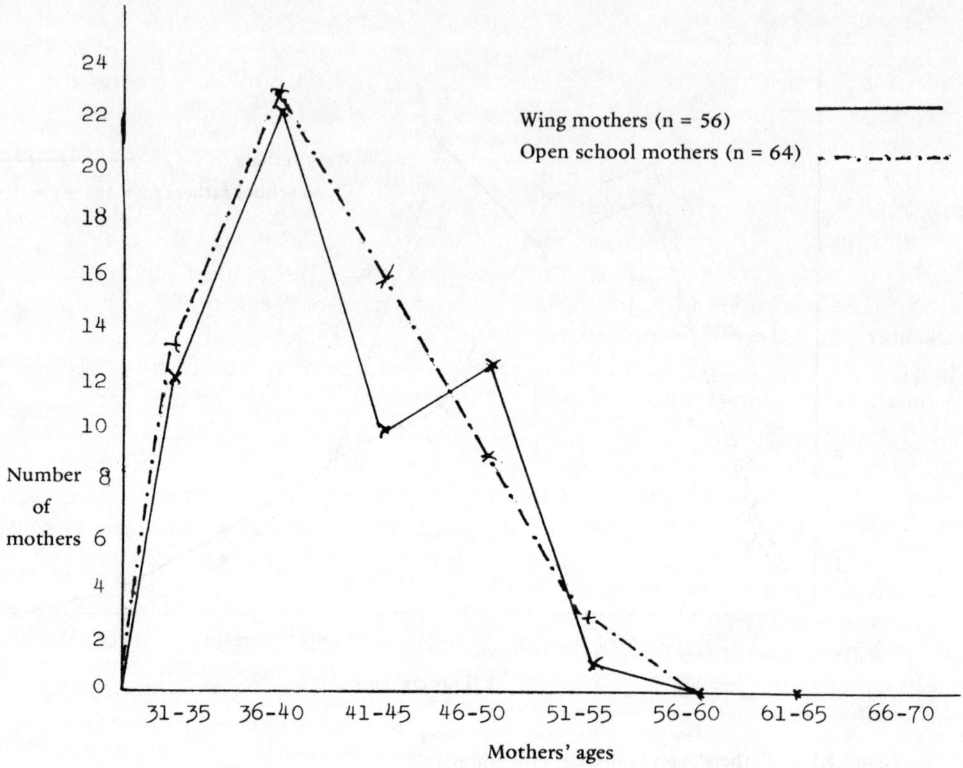

Figure 3.10 Mothers' ages in both groups compared

Table 3.23

Mothers' ages in both groups compared

Age	31-35	36-40	41-45	46-50	51-55	56-60	61-65
Wing (n = 56)	10	22	10	13	1	0	0
Open school (n = 64)	13	23	16	9	3	0	0

't' = 0.16, df = 108, p 0.20 (no significant difference)

Age of natural parents

It was not possible to find the ages of all natural parents at the time the boys were in Forest, either from the boys' files or from their own accounts. As will be already apparent, only information about the stable intact families is present for both parents, and for the parents who stayed with their children, either as remarried or single, and even for them precise age information is not always available. Ages can be a cherished secret, boys not knowing their parents' ages, and social enquiry reports sometimes not containing the information. Nevertheless, it seemed of interest to look at the information which is available.

Figures 3.7 and 3.8 and Tables 3.20 and 3.21 show that in both groups mothers are significantly younger than fathers, as would be expected, since this is so in the normal population. Most mothers appear to be between thirty-six and forty years of age. Fathers are older, the mode being between forty and fifty, and ages more widely spaced than the mothers'. Ten fathers are over fifty in the Wing and eight in the Open school. There are only four mothers of this age, to be expected as fertility for women drops after age forty. With the average age of the boys being fifteen, no mothers over fifty-five would be expected.

Parents, with sons of between fourteen and sixteen, will be middle aged, as in the normal population. There is therefore nothing notable in regard to their ages and those of their sons which might be considered cause for disturbed and deviant behaviour. Sons will be born to mothers in their twenties and to fathers somewhat older. Even the 18 fathers of over fifty will have been in their late thirties when their sons were born.

Fathers' ages in both groups compared (Figure 3.9 and Table 3.22)

The graph appears to show that the Wing fathers are older than the Open school fathers. Analysis by 't' test corrects this impression as no significant difference appears. Nevertheless, the graph makes the point that 18 Wing boys and only 8 Open school boys have fathers in the late forties. This discrepancy disappears when the ages are seen overall.

The average age of fathers in the Wing is 44.05 years and 42.77 years for the Open school fathers. This difference is not significant.

Mothers' ages in both groups compared (Figure 3.10 and Table 3.23)

This graph also appears to show discrepancy, not borne out by the 't' test analysis which reveals no significant difference.

The mean age of the Wing mothers is 41.27 years and that of the Open school mothers 39.88 years.

Summary

Ages of parents in both groups have no significant differences. Distribution is similar to that in the normal population, with mothers younger than fathers.

Religion

It was considered of interest to enquire if mixed religions in mother and father had an influence on the boy's rearing, for the religious divisions between Roman Catholics and Protestants might have been disruptive to the families. In the outcome this did not appear to be so. Ten families in the Wing had mixed religions and five in the Open school. This is not a significant difference (see Table 3.24). Nor did the boys consider the different religions in their parents to be important when this was discussed with them. No strong religious feeling appeared to affect the boys personally and church seemed a matter of indifference. Two boys in the Wing said they were Orangemen like their older brothers, and appeared to regard this as being part of a 'gang' and not of a religion. They considered the Orange Walk in Glasgow as a high point of the year, when carnival (and fights) took place.

Table 3.24

Religion of parents

	Wing (n = 100)	Open school (n = 100)	Chi-square test	Level of significance
Protestant	33	53	$x^2 = 8.1501$, df = 1, $p < 0.01$	0.01
Catholic	22	9	$x^2 = 6.451$, df = 1, $0.05 > p > 0.02$	0.05
	32	14		
Mixed marriages	10	5	$x^2 = 1.8018$, df = 1 $p > 0.10$	n.s.
None	35	33	–	n.s.
TOTAL	100	100		

No religious divisions appeared between the boys. Friends were made by home territory, not religion. Even boys who had been reared in Roman Catholic List D schools since childhood appeared indifferent. Mass was said weekly in the Wing, which boys appeared to attend as a parade.

The number of Roman Catholics in the Wing is significantly higher than in the Open school, seeming to produce a real difference between the groups in this dimension (significant at the 0.05 level). But on reflection this is not valid because the Open school is mainly for Protestant boys and the Wing is undenominational.

Summary of family data

Table 3.25 summarises the comparisons of family situations for each group.

Table 3.25
Summary

	Wing	Open school	Tests of comparative difference	Level of significance
Family size	5.18 children	4.79 children	't' = 1.18, df = 198 $p > 0.10$	n.s.
Delinquent siblings	45	37	$x^2 = 1.01$, df = 1, $p > 0.10$	n.s.
Boy's birth rank in family	mode 3rd child	mode 3rd child	–	–
Intact families	55	50	$x^2 = 0.50$, df = 1, $p > 0.10$	n.s.
Second partner families	21	21	–	–
Father remarried	6	5	–	n.s.
Mother remarried	15	16	–	–
Single parent families	23	27	$x^2 = 0.43$, df = 1, $p > 0.10$	n.s.
Single parent father	6	10	$x^2 = 1.00$, df = 1, $p > 0.10$	n.s.
Single parent mother	17	17	–	n.s.

Table 3.25 (continued)

	Wing	Open school	Tests of comparative difference	Level of significance
Broken families	45	50	$x^2 = 0.51$, df = 1, $p > 0.10$	n.s.
Both parents lost	1 }	2 }	–	n.s.
Mother lost	12 } 45	15 } 50	$x^2 = 0.39$, df = 1, $p > 0.10$	n.s.
Father lost	32 }	33 }	–	n.s.
Intact families, employed fathers	29/55	36/50	$x^2 = 1.12$, df = 1, $p > 0.10$	n.s.
Intact families, employed mothers	21/55	29/50	$x^2 = 1.71$, df = 1, $p > 0.10$	n.s.
Handicapped fathers and unemployed	23/55	12/50	$x^2 = 4.19$, df = 1, $0.05 > p > 0.01$	0.05
Housewife mothers	34/55	20/50	$x^2 = 4.97$, df = 1, $0.05 > p > 0.01$	0.05
Handicapped mothers	0/55	1/50	–	–
Unemployed fathers 'fit'	3/55	2/50	–	–
Non-wage contributing fathers	68	62	$x^2 = 1.076$, df = 1, $p > 0.01$	n.s.
Stepmothers	6	5	–	–
Stepfathers	15	16	–	–
Single parent fathers in employment	6	10	$x^2 = 1.09$, df = 1, $p > 0.10$	n.s.
Deserting mothers	1	7	–	–
Single parent mothers	17	17	–	n.s.
Single mothers in employment	4	7	–	n.s.
Age at loss of parent (father or mother or both)	mode is age 8.5	mode is age 7.5	$x^2 = 0.16$, df = 93, $p > 0.20$	n.s.
Age at loss of mother	mode is 9 years	mode is 9 years	't' = 0.45, df = 28 $p > 0.10$	n.s.

Table 3.25 (continued)

	Wing	Open school	Test of comparative difference	Level of significance
Parents lost (father or mother)	45	50	$x^2 = 0.51$, df = 1 $p > 0.10$	n.s.
Illegitimacy	1	5	–	n.s.
Death of parents (total)	9	6	$x^2 = 0.65$, df = 1, $p > 0.10$	n.s.
Death of mothers	4	2	–	n.s.
Death of fathers	5	4	–	n.s.
Age of mothers (mean years)	41.27	39.88	't' = 0.16, df = 108, $p > 0.20$	n.s.
Age of natural fathers (mean years)	44.05	42.77	't' = 0.16, df = 112, $p > 0.20$	n.s.
Catholic	22	9	$x^2 = 6.451$, df = 1, $0.02 > p > 0.01$	0.02
Protestants	33	53	$x^2 = 8.1501$, df = 1, $p > 0.01$	0.01
Mixed marriages	10	5	$x^2 = 1.8018$, df = 1, $p > 0.10$	n.s.
No religion	35	33	–	n.s.

Conclusion

The two groups of boys are homogeneous throughout this catalogue of family situations and are significantly different in three categories only: handicapped fathers, housewife mothers and religion.

4 Previous placements

The List D school system can sometimes be looked upon as a network where the pattern is made by children who pass through. Junior schools often feed to the intermediate, the intermediate to senior schools, with the last resort being the closed units, at present the Carpenter Wing of Forest School and the Merchant Wing of another intermediate List D school. Some children drop out of the system, released from their first school and not reappearing. Others, after release, commit further offences, go to a Hearing, or a Court, and return either to their former school, or elsewhere. Some schools discourage return of pupils even if the age range is still acceptable since a former pupil can be disruptive to a situation which has changed since he left and now involves a new group of children. This may not be what is envisaged in the Social Work (Scotland) Act 1970 which expected List D schools to become part of a range of local authority resources but it is the case at present.

Transfer also sometimes occurs but not so frequently in Scotland as Millham et al. (1977) appear to find in their research on CHEs (Community Homes with Education on the premises) in England. Usually if a child persistently absconds or is unmanageable (or 'too bloody minded' in residential vernacular) he finds himself in an assessment centre or Longriggend*, a 'place of safety', and there awaits a Hearing and reallocation under the aegis of his social worker. The child can be placed in an assessment centre summarily when apprehended by Police if he has absconded, or by the consent of the Director of Social Work if the school cannot contain him. In this situation a Hearing must be convened within seven days. An 'unruly certificate' from the Court is necessary before a placement in a penal establishment can be made and then only if the child is facing a charge laid in the Sheriff Court. Table 4.6 analyses such penal placements.

Prisons are unwilling to hold children and transfer them as quickly as possible elsewhere, but in Longriggend or an assessment centre there are some children for whom social workers cannot find a 'vacancy'—a 'vackie' in the childrens' language—and their period in such limbo stretches out gloomily. The List D world is a small one and a child with a bad reputation as 'difficult' can be 'labelled' so that no school wants him. There are, however, some headmasters who enjoy the challenge of such a child but

*A section of Barlinnie, the Glasgow prison, reserved for offenders under 21 and for boys under 16 on an 'unruly certificate' or awaiting placement after sentence.

staff need to be considered. The 'bad apple in the barrel', they say, 'can spoil the lot'. Some such children, whom no school will accept, find themselves for long periods in assessment centres, or very occasionally a penal establishment although these latter children are given priority for placing. If a school can be found to take them quickly they are lucky if Longriggend is the placement, but some children can settle in assessment centres contentedly. Indeed some assessment centres claim that they can successfully care for children with whom List D schools have failed.

Hearings tend to place children as close as possible to their homes for ease of travel and liaison with parents and social workers. Nevertheless, because of pressure for places, many children from the west of Scotland are placed in the east and north east List D schools since it is from the densely populated west that most children derive.

Strathclyde region has half the population of Scotland and contains severely depressed socioeconomic areas where large sectors of the population are unemployed due to the decline of the heavy industries, shipbuilding, iron and steel works, which caused its high prosperity in the nineteenth century. The population of Glasgow has declined greatly since its heyday of 1½ million to some 800,000. Those people who remain find work opportunity has diminished, creating conditions of deprivation which seem to correlate with crime. Thus Forest, some one hundred miles from Strathclyde and very inaccessible for transport, has many boys from there (see Figure 6.2).

Sometimes the Hearings deliberately place a boy far from his native home if he is frequently absconding in order to make his return home less easy, in the hope that he will 'settle' in the List D school to which he was allocated.

Forest Open school boys

Forest Open school, like other senior schools, is the recipient of boys making their way through the List D system, as well as of boys on their first placement. Table 4.1 demonstrates this process and shows all the List D schools for boys in Scotland, giving their populations. These numbers fall and rise seasonally. The figures given are the official top limit for each school at the time of this study in 1978. The number of ex-boys from each of the schools in Forest are ranked in order.

The age of entry is approximate, for the headmaster has some discretion in accepting (or refusing) boys.

The geographical influence of interdigitation between schools

Obviously List D schools with large populations will have greater numbers

Table 4.1

Former List D schools of boys in Forest Open school (n = 100)

(rank order)

	School	Total population of boys	Number of ex-pupils in Forest
M	School 1 (Intermediate)*	100	9
P	School 2 (Junior)*	82	8
P	School 3 (Intermediate)*	104	8
P	School 4 (Intermediate)	90	3
P	School 5 (Intermediate)	40	3
P	School 6 (Senior)	77	2
P	School 7 (Junior)	30	2
P	School 8 (Junior)	71	3
M	School 9 (Junior)*	23	1
RC	School 10 (Junior)	80	1
RC	School 11 (Senior)	78	1
RC	School 12 (Senior)	80	1
P	School 13 (Senior)	60	0
P	School 14 (Senior)	110	0
P	School 15 (Intermediate/Senior)	46	0
RC	School 16 (Intermediate)	95	0
RC	School 17 (Senior)	50	0
RC	School 18 (Junior/Intermediate)	90	0
RC	School 19 (Junior/Intermediate)	24	0
M	Forest	90	–

*Neighbouring schools to Forest

Grade	Age on entry	Religion
Senior	14½ years	RC – Roman Catholic
Intermediate/ Senior	13+ years but under 15 years	P – Protestant
Junior/Inter-mediate	11½–13½ years	M – Mixed
Junior	under 13½ years	

of boys who go on to further compulsory residential establishments than smaller schools. Also schools remote from Forest will be represented by fewer boys, save in exceptional circumstances, their local senior schools absorbing their recidivist children. Table 4.1 shows this pattern.

School 1, an intermediate school of some 100 boys situated close to Forest, has 9 boys in Forest Open school. School 2, a junior school also of 100 boys and also geographically close, has almost the same number.

School 3, a Protestant junior school of 82 boys in Edinburgh, also has ex-pupils in Forest Open school (8 boys), in that Forest is the main non-Catholic List D school in the east of Scotland. Such consistent numbers indicate that about 10 per cent of junior and intermediate boys in geographically neighbouring schools proceed to Forest Open school. The table also shows the diminishing number of boys from schools proportionally distant from Forest Open school.

The effect of transfer or reconviction and placement in a different school

The Dartington Social Research Unit's research (Millham, Bullock, Hosie and Frankenberg, 1977) into the prognosis for pupils after changes of school should have an influence on Hearings considering placement, for it found that the prospects for a boy deteriorate after moving from one school to another. In this present study 44 places in 12 other different schools have been occupied by the 100 Forest Open school boys in the past, some boys having been in more than one (see Table 4.1). They have either been transferred or sent home and have been in trouble again and sent to further compulsory residential placement.

Analysing the number of placements in List D schools for each boy, previous to coming to the Open Forest School, revealed that 66 boys had not been in a List D school beforehand. 25 boys had one previous school, 8 had two and only one boy had been in three schools. Figure 4.1 shows this graphically and as a table.

The level of previous placement in List D schools is therefore not high although, as we shall find out later in this study, all but 23 of the boys have been in various other institutions (detailed later in Figure 4.4).

The 'labelling' system is starting for all of them, by the very fact of conviction (Farrington and West 1977) and for the boys in repeat convictions the 'old lag' syndrome begins to grow: they must adapt to new rules, new staff, a new peer group, a new way of life—for each List D school, as any institution, has a way of its own. The boys become institutionalised as they move from one to another. Schools which keep their boys (say Millham et al, 1977 and 1978) have the best hope of helping them in the long term, as have those who receive them back again if they offend after release.

One major difficulty in keeping and receiving a boy back again after a further conviction is the policy of some schools that it is better to have boys of similar ages together and thus maintain some degree of peer equality. Older and younger boys in institutions do not, it is felt, mix well nor live together well. It would seem each remedy brings its own disadvantage.

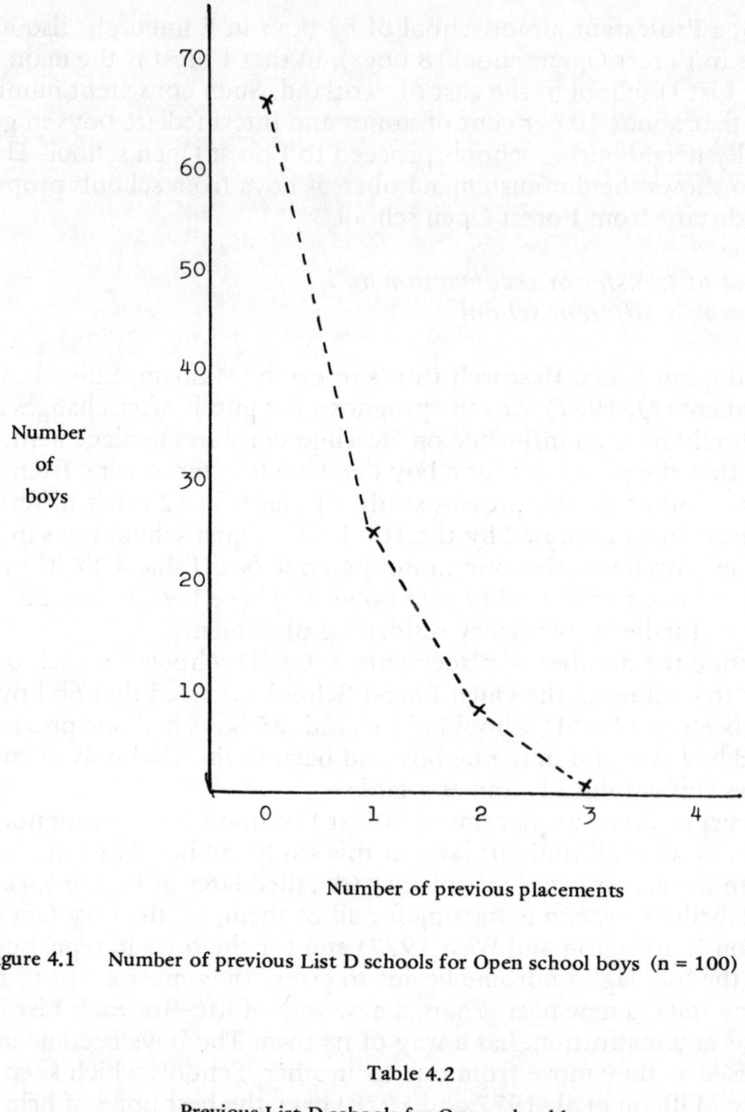

Figure 4.1 Number of previous List D schools for Open school boys (n = 100)

Table 4.2

Previous List D schools for Open school boys

Number of previous schools	0	1	2	3	4
Open school boys (n = 100)	66	25	8	1	0

Summary

In short, 66 boys in the Open school have no previous experience in a List D school, although only 23 of these were innocent of previous institutional experience such as assessment centres, childrens' homes, foster homes, hospitals, etc. (see Figure 4.4). The impact of the strangeness of residential compulsory care is severe to the new boys. The boys with previous List D experience are 'old hands' and are often fulfilling the labelling prediction. Two thirds are in the first condition, one third in the latter, among the Open school boys in this study.

The Carpenter Wing and its boys

The above discussion of the boys in the open part of Forest School leads to that of those in the Wing, the high security unit. The Wing was opened in 1962 and was a 'pilot' scheme for which the authorities had no previous experience in Britain or indeed in Europe. It was planned nearly a decade before the Social Work (Scotland) Act 1968 and has now been in operation for seventeen years (1962–79).

The Wing is connected by an open corridor to the Open school and has the same headmaster, but the day to day control is the responsibility of the deputy headmaster. The Open school does not have window bars and the front door is not locked. The Wing is totally secure and is always locked. The population of the Wing is small, 20 to 24 boys. At the time of this research the Open school held between 80–90 boys depending on demand. The reputation of the Wing, promoted by the other schools, is as a 'bogy' for recalcitrant and absconding boys and used to be sinister. At one time few people, save staff, officials and the occasional parent, ever visited. It was an unknown quantity. Boys in other schools feared it, and residential care staff in other establishments held similar prejudices.

Yet many boys who have been in the Wing remember their time there with affection and keep in touch with staff for many years after release. Very great child care skills are in operation between staff and boys, little known except to the pupils, and not publicised. The present research is endeavouring to redress the esoteric situation of the Wing, in relation to the nature of its boys. A description of the psychological conditions for both sets of boys is not germane to the present study and may be undertaken in a further work.

It is possible that the dark reputation of the Wing spreads over the Open school itself and Hearings and Courts sending boys to Forest School see it as prodromal to the Wing under whose shadow Forest lies in the List D system's mythology and also in the mythology of social workers, police and the public. It is important in this regard to note that only one major incident has occurred in the Wing and that in 1964 in its earliest days.

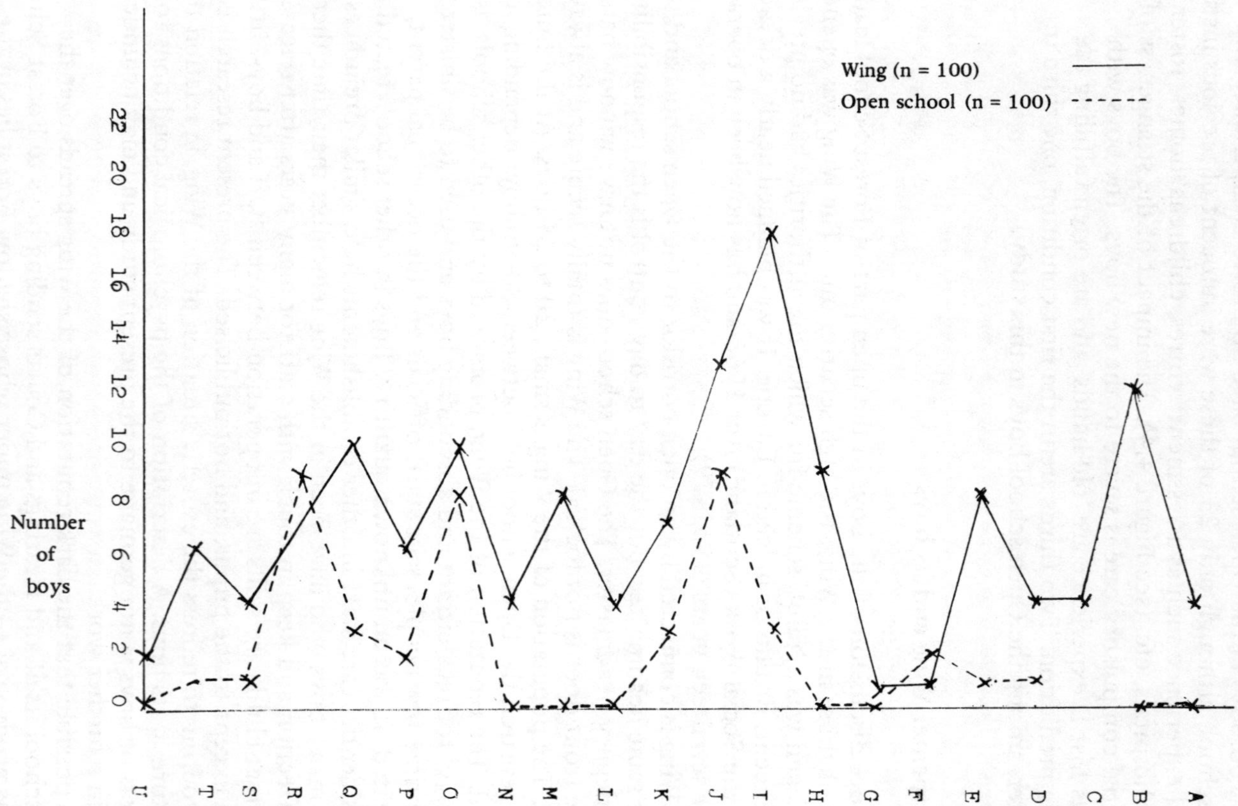

Figure 4.2 Previous List D schools–both groups (Forest School not applicable)

Until recently, therefore, List D schools from all over Scotland funnelled their most difficult boys, however few in number, into the Wing. In 1975 a further high security unit, the Merchant Wing, was opened. It is attached to a Roman Catholic school for boys of intermediate age, thirteen to fourteen and a half. The Merchant Wing, like the Carpenter Wing, shares the same headmaster as the parent 'open' school. In planning and philosophy it reflects the experience of the most modern social work thinking.

Liaison between the two secure units is developing by exchange visits of staff and an assessment team of heads, deputy heads, psychologists, psychiatrists, social workers and an adviser from SWSG now deliberate on the selection of some of the boys for placement in each unit.

Analysis of former List D placements for the two groups of boys

Chapter 2 found there was little statistical difference between the groups in terms of offences. Chapter 3 found only three significant differences. Is the number of previous schools the significant reason for high security placement for the Wing boys?

Figure 4.2 and Table 4.3 show the number of boys in our study from the various List D schools in Scotland in the Wing and in the Open school. The picture vividly brings to the understanding that in nearly every case more boys from each school are in the Wing than in the Open school. The comparative naivety of the Open school boys in terms of residential experience is not mirrored in the Wing boys.

Former List D schools and the Wing boys

Delving more deeply, it appeared of interest to show which schools supplied most boys to the Wing. Table 4.4 gives this in rank order. It should be noted that the rank order of ex-pupils from other schools in the Wing is different from that in the Open school.

Further, some pupils have been in more than one school, in 'homes', in hospitals, also in several assessment centres, Longriggend or prisons. These placements are counted in Table 2.3.

It is of interest that some junior and junior intermediate schools have few boys who continue in the List D ladder to the Wing. Millham et al. (1977), quoted above, recommend early therapeutic intervention. This, it appears from the data here presented, is shown as occurring effectively in the Scottish system in some cases.

Larger schools will predicate more recidivist children in that more children proportionately will stay in the List D system.

School I. This is an intermediate school of excellent reputation, with a nominal population of 90 boys, and it has the largest number of boys in the Wing. It seemed of interest to analyse the past history in terms of previous placements of these boys. Table 4.5 illuminates their stories, showing the diversity of past experiences and establishments each in turn for the boys.

Table 4.3

Random frequency of boys from List D schools in the Open school and Wing

Former school	Population of school	Number of ex-pupils in Wing	Number of ex-pupils in Open school
Senior			
A	60	4	0
B	110	12	0
C	90	4	not applicable
D	78	4	1
E	80	8	1
Senior/intermediate			
F	77	1	2
G	46	1	0
Intermediate			
H	95	9	0
I	90	18	3
J	100	13	9
K	40	7	3
Junior/intermediate			
L	50	4	0
M	90	8	0
N	24	4	0
Junior			
O	104	10	8
P	50	7	2
Q	71	10	3
R	82	9	8
S	23	4	1
T	80	6	1

Table 4.4
Frequency of pupils from former schools in the Wing (rank order)

Former school		Population of school	Number of ex-pupils in the Wing
I	(intermediate)	90	18
J	(intermediate)	100	13
B	(senior)	110	12
Q	(junior)	71	10
O	(junior)	104	10
H	(intermediate)	95	9
R	(junior	82	9
C	(senior)	90	8
F	(senior)	80	8
M	(junior/intermediate)	90	8
K	(intermediate)	40	7
P	(junior)	50	7
T	(junior)	80	6
D	(senior)	78	4
L	(junior/intermediate)	50	4
N	(junior/intermediate)	24	4
S	(junior)	23	4
A	(senior)	60	4
F	(senior)	77	1
G	(senior/intermediate)	46	1

Table 4.5

Previous placements of each pupil in the Wing from School *I*
(highest ranking in Table 4.4/or boys in the Wing having 18 ex-boys there)

Pupil	Schools	Assessment centres	Other
1	School *I* Junior List D school Intermediate List D school	Two assessment centres	Longriggend
2	School *I* (accepted back continuously after many abscondings to England with offences there)	–	Saughton Prison
3	School *I* (20 abscondings)		
4	Junior List D school School *I*	Assessment centre	Longriggend
5	Junior List D school School *I* Senior List D school	Assessment centre (many abscondings)	
6	Junior List D school School *I*	Children's home Two assessment centres	Longriggend
7	School *I*	Two assessment centres	Longriggend
8	Junior List D school School *I*	Two assessment centres	Psychiatric hospital
9	School *I* Intermediate List D school	–	–
10	School *I*	Assessment centre	
11	Junior List D school School *I*	Two assessment centres	Children's home Longriggend
12	Two junior List D schools School *I*	Assessment centre	–
13	School *I* Intermediate List D school	Assessment centre	Longriggend
14	School *I* Senior List D school	–	Children's home School for maladjusted Longriggend
15	School *I*	Assessment centre	Longriggend
16	School *I*	Assessment centre	Longriggend Cromlin Road Jail
17	School *I*	Two assessment centres	–
18	Junior List D school	Two assessment centres	Children's home

In aggregate these 18 boys now in the Wing and at one time on the roll of School *I* have collected 68 placements over their history in institutions. Examination of the table shows children's homes, psychiatric hospitals, hostels, assessment centres in plenty, junior and intermediate and even senior List D schools. Longriggend and prisons also feature—the gamut of institutional provision.

School *I* was only one stopping place in this progress and the tolerance School *I* shows in accepting back absconders (e.g. up to twenty times—cases 2 and 3) should be noted.

The same analysis was carried out for School *J* also an intermediate Protestant school of 100 boys aged thirteen and a half to fifteen years with similar results (see Table 4.6).

Table 4.6
Previous schools of each boy now in the Wing in School *J* (intermediate)

	Schools	Assessment centres	Others
1	School *J* Junior List D school	Assessment centre	Longriggend
2	School *J*	Assessment centre	Longriggend
3	School *J*	Assessment centre	Longriggend
4	Junior List D school Intermediate List D school	Assessment centre	Prison
5	School *J*	Assessment centre	Prison
6	School *J*	Assessment centre	–
7	School *J*	School for maladjusted	Children's home
8	School *J*	–	Longriggend Prison
9	Junior List D school	Two assessment centres	Prison
10	Junior List D school School *J*	–	Longriggend Prison
11	School *J*	Assessment centre	Prison Children's home
12	Junior List D school School *J*	Assessment centre	Longriggend
13	School *J* Junior List D school	Assessment centre	–

The 13 boys in the Wing who have at one time been on the role of School J have 45 previous placements in the same variety as the former School I boys. The average number of placements for these Wing boys in both schools is around five.

It is therefore clear that neither school carries responsibility for any one boy, for many other establishments are involved as the boys continue to offend and collect institutional placements from Hearings and Courts, before eventually landing in a high security unit, the Wing. The high level of boys in the Wing from both schools indicates the broad-mindedness of these schools in accepting boys whom they know to be difficult from their case histories.

Penal placements, Longriggend and prisons

In addition to other institutions, some boys in both groups have had periods in the penal system. Such have been deemed 'unruly' by the procurator fiscal and are given an 'unruly certificate'. They can thereafter be held on a remand order in a penal establishment. Longriggend is the main holding place for boys under sixteen years. A number of Strathclyde boys have been placed there as the main remand prison in the region but boys from other regions are also placed there. Adult prisons throughout Scotland are also occasionally used for temporary remand purposes, transferring the boy as quickly as possible to Longriggend on remand.

Table 4.7 shows the number of boys in the study from the Wing and the Open school who have been in specific prisons. Longriggend has held 40 of the 100 Wing boys and 10 of the Open school boys—a significant difference (see Table 4.7). Other Scottish prisons have also been used but for small numbers of boys.

Table 4.7

Penal placements of boys before entry (Longriggend and prison)

Placement	Wing	Open school	Chi-square test	Level of significance
Longriggend	40	10	$x^2 = 22.73$, df = 1, $0.001 > p$	0.001 (highly significant)
Saughton Prison	4	2	–	–
Barlinnie Prison	3	1	–	–
Craiginches Prison	3	1	–	–
Perth Prison	1	3	–	–
Porterfield Prison	2	0	–	–
Cromlin Road Jail	1	0	–	–
Glenochil Detention Centre	1	0	–	–
TOTAL	55	16	$x^2 = 33.2132$, df = 1, $0.001 > p$	0.001 (highly significant)

Longriggend is part of the penal system, holding boys up to age twenty-one. School boys (under sixteen) are lodged apart from older boys, but in conditions patently penal. To the layman, and to many social workers, the conditions are shocking. High fences surround the institution. Boys can emerge bewildered and hardened, and recovery to normal adolescent thinking is slow. 'Doing your Long' nominates a boy into the juvenile criminal world. Haircut, prison pallor and the automatic use of 'sir' are its insignia.

It is bizarre that some boys are not convicted but still merely on remand, placed there on emergency admission on an 'unruly certificate' until a Court appearance.

Adult prisons also receive boys but only short term. In Longriggend, however, boys may stay for some time depending on the date of their Court hearing. After sentence they become the responsibility of the Secretary of State and if placement is outside the penal system, which it usually is, priority is accorded to them. Adult prisons transfer the boys as rapidly as maybe to Longriggend for children are an embarrassment to them and questions in Parliament may be asked of all concerned. The Criminal Procedure (Scotland) Act 1975 lays down in Section 415: 'No Court shall impose imprisonment on a person under seventeen years of age'.

The experience of Longriggend for a child is indefensible to minds geared to the spirit of Kilbrandon and social work theory. It is, however, encouraging to see that the numbers placed in penal establishments by Courts under 'unruly certificates' have dropped considerably over the past year (1978) to well under 200, and children under sixteen placed long term in any penal establishment are very few in number compared to the rest of Britain taking into account population differences. This says much about the capacity of the List D schools to 'absorb' difficult children.

Wing boys and Open school boys and their previous placements. The files of all the boys were searched to discover all their previous placements in institutions, including children's homes, schools for maladjusted children, psychiatric hospitals, List D schools, foster homes, hostels, assessment centres and Longriggend (see Figure 2.1). Statistical analysis shows the mean and standard deviations of the number of previous placements for both groups (see Table 4.7).

Table 4.8

Mean previous placements of the boys in both groups

	Wing boys (n = 100)	Open school boys (n = 100)
Mean previous placements	3.54	1.56
Standard deviation	1.47	1.33
TOTAL	100	100

The difference between the means for the two groups is highly significant ('t' = 9.90, df = 198, $p < 0.001$). This means that the Wing boys have many more previous placements of all types than the Open school boys.

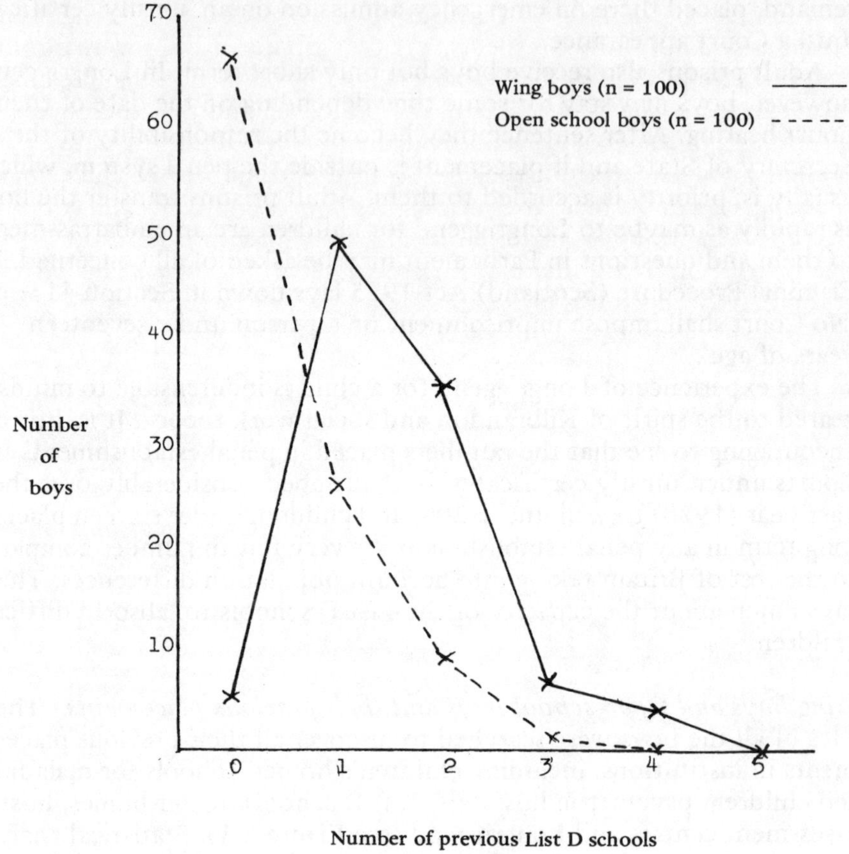

Figure 4.3 Previous List D schools compared

Number of previous List D schools	0	1	2	3	4	5
Wing boys (n = 100)	5	49	35	7	4	0
Open school boys (n = 100)	66	25	8	1	0	0

Wing boys have more List D placements than Open school boys ('t' = 10.18, df = 198, $p < 0.001$) highly significant difference

It is with special interest that this highly significant difference is now noted as so far, in other respects, the two groups of boys were homogeneous save in the finding that the Wing boys had more handicapped fathers and housewife mothers at the 0.05 level and that there were differences of religious adherence at the 0.05 level in the groups. This present highly significant measure of difference in previous placements is of special importance. It confirms the impression conveyed subjectively that the Wing boys are different in that they have moved restlessly from one institution to another and finally arrived at the Wing. This difference is the first discovered in this study which relates to the boys themselves and not to their family situations.

Number of previous List D schools for each individual boy in both groups compared. Following the study of the aggregate of institutional placements for each of the boys in the two groups, an examination of the previous List D schools for each individual boy was undertaken, contrasting this analysis with that of Table 4.1 when aggregates of schools' ex-pupils were examined. Table 4.9 and Figure 4.3 show the situation concerning previous List D placements for both groups. It will again be seen that there are highly significant differences between the number of previous List D placements for the Wing boys and the Open school boys.

Table 4.9

Previous List D schools compared

Number of List D schools	Wing (n = 100)	Open school (n = 100)	Chi-square test	Level of significance
0	5	66	$x^2 = 81.2534$, df = 1, $p < 0.001$	0.001
1	49	25	$x^2 = 12.3552$, df = 1, $p < 0.001$	0.001
2	35	8	$x^2 = 21.5968$, df = 1, $p < 0.001$	0.001
3	7	1	–	–
4	4	0	–	–
TOTAL	100	100		

Further analysis by 't' test finds a highly significant difference 't' = 10.18, df = 198, $p < 0.001$.

Wing boys (n = 100) and Open school boys (n = 100) without previous List D placements compared. Figure 4.3 and Table 4.9 show that five Wing boys and 66 Open school boys had not previously been in List D schools. The zero List D boys in each group were therefore examined in turn.

Wing boys without previous List D placements (n = 5). Analysis of the previous histories of the five boys who had not previously been in a List D school discovered the following information on their earlier placements.

Case 1 Assessment centre
Detention centre
Prison
Longriggend

Case 2 Assessment centre
Longriggend—a 206(2) case

Case 3 Assessment centre (twice)
Longriggend

Case 4 Assessment centre
Detention centre
Prison
Longriggend

Case 5 Three children's homes
Church of Scotland hostel
Assessment centre
(This boy is illegitimate. His mother died on 30 March 1976 and a month afterwards he was placed in an assessment centre.)

It is obvious how involved four boys have been with the penal side, Cases 1 and 4 in three penal institutions and Cases 1, 2, 3 and 4 in Longriggend (a penal institution) as well as assessment centres. The fifth boy has passed his youth 'in care'. There are therefore no boys in the Wing, even in the zero previous List D school group, with no previous institutional experience.

Open school boys without previous List D placements. The Open school boys who have not been in List D schools were examined next; of these there were 66. Nevertheless, some had previous institutional placements (see Table 4.10). Their experiences, however, appear less harsh.

It would be cumberous to analyse individually the experiences of each of the 66 boys as has been done for the five Wing boys. They are therefore grouped in Table 4.11 to give information on their past placement histories.

Table 4.10

Open school boys with no previous List D placement (n = 66)

Number of placements	Number of boys
0	23
1	25
2	13
3	5
TOTAL	66

Table 4.11

Details of placements for Open school boys

Placement	Number of boys		Number of previous placements
No previous placement, i.e. direct from home	23		0
Assessment centres	21		
Children's home or shelter	2	25	1
Longriggend	1		
Prison	1		
Assessment centre and Longriggend			
Assessment centre and boys' hostel			
Prison and assessment centre			
Two assessment centres			
Two assessment centres			
Assessment centre and foster home			
Prison and assessment centre	13		2
Assessment centre and hostel			
Prison and Longriggend			
Children's home and assessment centre			
Prison and assessment centre			
Children's shelter and children's home			
Children's home and assessment centre			
Assessment centre, psychiatric hospital, children's home			
Two assessment centres and children's home			
Assessment centre, children's home and Longriggend	5		3 each
Assessment centre, children's home and hostel			
Two assessment centres, Longriggend			
TOTAL	66		

Egregious in the boys with only one previous placement are the two boys who had been in prison and Longriggend. The Longriggend boy was convicted on a charge of 'serious assault' in company with other boys on an elderly drunken man in a Glasgow 'vennel' who, he said, had initiated the affray. He had received a Section 206(2) sentence. The other was a strange introverted boy, from a family where mother had left and whose 'unemployed' father had brought up the five children. Indeed the placement in School C was unusual in that he attained his sixteenth birthday ten days before his Court appearance (Borstal entry age) and might well have been placed there. The initial psychological report on this boy is reproduced here in order to describe him.

Report (2 April 1976)

John is a boy from Aberdeen. He is most profoundly depressed and were it not that he was going on leave on Monday, extreme concern might be justifiably felt in his regard. He is a boy who has withdrawn into himself and feels afflicted with absolute despair by his removal from home. He has now been in Forest for six weeks, and the intense gloom has not lifted. He finds the enforced intimacy with strangers intolerable, and has made no overtures to make friends. He feels himself the object of quite considerable harassment from other boys.

John's present state is not new to him in that he started to truant from school in his first year because he believed that he was being persecuted by teachers in the school. His paranoia is always close to the surface, but more markedly so now in this translation from home to compulsory residential care.

John's mother left the family home taking only one daughter of the family with her. She is now cohabiting with another partner and has two children of this new union. John's father, who is unemployed, has looked after the remaining children, five in number. An older boy has just returned from Borstal, and John said gloomily that the brother had been charged with assault, but had never spoken about it because it was 'something he did not like to speak about'. John added however that his brother had learnt to cook in the Borstal, and now was able to help his father with the preparation for meals in the family home.

John is particularly missing his father, but he says the father does not understand how important letters are to boys in Forest. He said that he did not wish his father to send him presents or parcels, because there was not enough money to do this. Concern and consideration for his father appeared on several occasions during the interview.

John's nature is obviously that of an introvert and an isolate, but he said 'everybody needs a friend sometimes'. On one such occasion, John went off with some friends to Paisley and, finding themselves without money to return home, effected several thefts. He was arrested in Paisley and taken to Court, and passed one night in prison, probably because his age was unknown. On the following day he was sentenced under Section 413 to two years' training. John is afflicted with a stutter which, although not severe, does hamper his communication. His deep depression is accentuated by the stutter, and by his way of looking down and avoiding eye contact. However, as the interview proceeded, he began to look directly at me and a little life appeared in his face. At the end of the interview he was talking volubly and expressing his distress at his exile from his home. He compared himself with the other boys in Forest, in that he had never been away from home before. Most other boys had been in previous List D schools and had people they had known earlier. Other boys came from districts where friends from their home area were also in Forest. He saw himself as the only boy from Aberdeen and although he knew that there was a boy from Dyce, which is near Aberdeen, he had not yet been able to talk with him. The sense of defeat and depression was very strong in John.

Recommendation

Further interviews with this boy on his return from the Easter holidays.

Boys with no List D school experience. Figure 4.4 illustrates the differences between the five boys in the Wing and the 66 boys in the Open school for those boys who have not been in a List D school previously.

The contrast between the two groups is very obvious with heavy weighting on the Wing boys in terms of previous placements before entry into the Wing.

The effect of residential institutions

The boys who have passed through several establishments as well as prison or Longriggend become 'institutionalised'. This word has various meanings, ranging from a zombie-like non-responsiveness, to a condition where a boy can manipulate the institution to satisfactorily serve his ends. 'Porridge', recently shown on BBC TV, provides an excellent example. Some boys have known scarcely any other life than that inside an institution. Some of the Wing boys have started residential placement at age eight in a junior List D school, probably placed there because of parental neglect. On release further 'trouble' leads him into an intermediate List D school and subsequently to one or more senior List D schools. Between schools he may remain in assessment centres until vacancies occur for him. In the various schools he meets children much like himself, and in the 'sorting places' of assessment centres many more. So when he arrives at the Wing he may already know half the boys there, and at least their brothers or cousins. In Scotland at any one time there are between 1,200 and 1,500 children in List D placement. This makes a population small enough for its members to be known to each other (indeed many normal comprehensive schools are in themselves larger units). By the time he has funnelled through the Wing and arrived at Borstal he will have a nodding knowledge of many of the inmates already there. Boyle (1978) and Meehan (1978), both recidivist criminals, describe the comforting, friendly greetings of inmates when they are returned to prisons—old comrades.

The euphemism used by the boys for any contact with the law is interesting. This is known as 'trouble' a portmanteau word with infinite connotations. Indeed, a private language used by institutionalised boys forms a protective mechanism in that legal terms are avoided and more 'comfortable' words used instead, and also words the boys understand. A study of the linguistics of 'compulsory measures of care', i.e. 'being sent away', 'doing time', could be of interest. The vocabulary used denotes belonging to a fraternity which has its own rules, ethos and vocabulary.

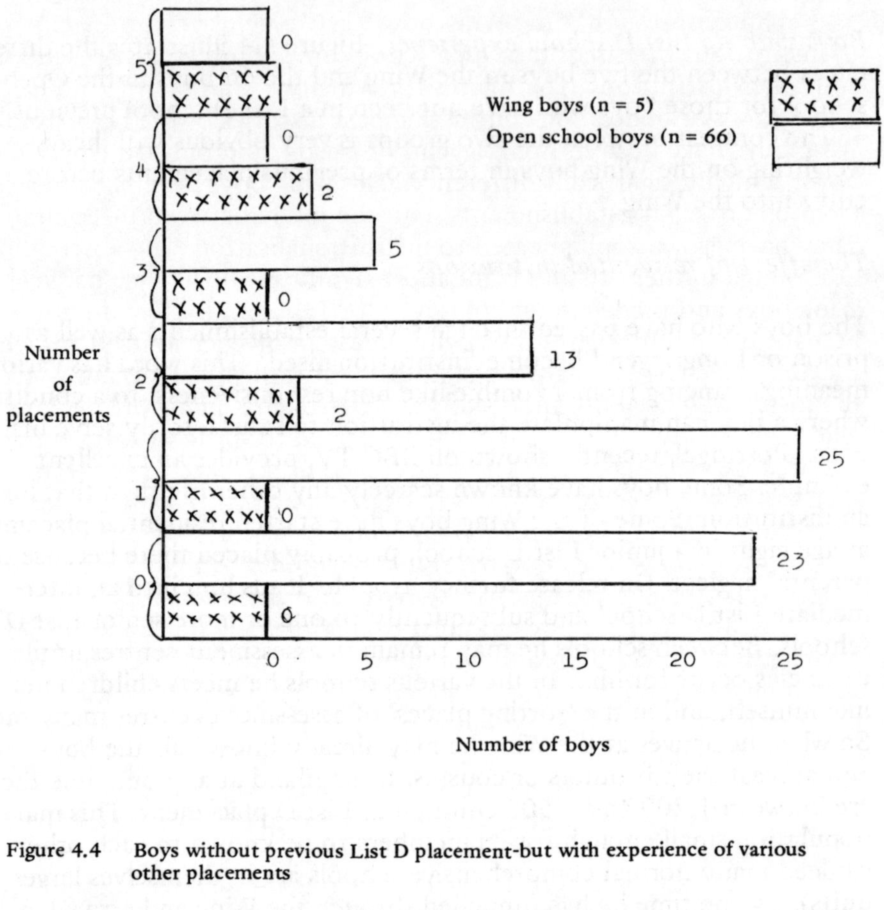

Figure 4.4 **Boys without previous List D placement-but with experience of various other placements**

Placements	0	1	2	3	4	5
Wing (n = 5)	0	0	2	0	2	1
Open school (n = 66)	23	25	13	5	0	0

Summary

This chapter shows that the Wing boys have conclusively more experience of institutional life than the Open school boys, both of List D schools and other institutions. The figures for Wing boys in Longriggend (see Table 4.7) symbolises the contrasting past histories of the boys, for 55 Wing boys have been in Longriggend or prison, and only 16 Open school boys—a highly significant difference. The Wing boys have been in a range from one to eight establishments with the mode between three and four. They have grown sophisticated to institutionalisation. The absconding rate is high in them all and is the most significant difference between the Wing boys and the Open school boys (see Table 2.2). They do not 'settle' in institutions and flight (absconding), not an offence in itself for which they can be charged, is always close to their thoughts. Once away from the institution they use their skills to 'live rough', 'living off the land' when 'on the run'. The vocabulary developed to speak of their experiences betrays their expertise. They have become an 'elite' group. Most know each other or of each other by way of previous List D schools, the sorting houses of assessment centres, Longriggend or prison. When they proceed, as most of them will, to Borstal, it will be almost to a club of acquaintances, relatives and friends. The 'circus' of the round of schools has become familiar to these boys, trained to institutional life. Indeed some have learned to rely on it and would be lost without the routine, the easy acceptance of food, clothing, shelter and the group living. The excitement of offences committed in the periods of freedom are expectedly bounded by further committals.

Finally, the reader is reminded that the number of placements does not correlate with the seriousness of the boys' offences which are not significantly different in nature or gravity—see Chapter 2.

It is a fair assumption from the evidence this study is accruing that the main reason for placement in the high security unit of the Wing is due to the factors of absconding and multiple previous placements. The offence of absconding from the establishment ordained by the Hearing or Court could perhaps be termed 'defeating the aims of justice' as the child is commanded in the committal order to 'obey the rules of the establishment'. Failure to do so creates secondary problems. It is therefore possible for a boy who has been placed in a List D school for failing to attend normal school (his only offence) and who subsequently absconds from List D schools, to have been in Longriggend and end up in the secure Wing. For boys who do commit offences before, during and after compulsory residential placements but refuse to stay for 'training', there is also the possibility of 'high security' placement.

5 Employment of parents and social class

Information about the occupations of the fathers of all boys in both groups was surprisingly difficult to gather. Little definite knowledge could be gained about the former jobs of handicapped and unemployed fathers, of the fathers of illegitimate sons, the deserting fathers, the dead and the long divorced. Social enquiry reports do not always dwell on this part of family history and the boys themselves often knew little as memory had faded or was vague.

However, the available information is set out in Table 5.1. This shows that there is no significant difference in the numbers of employed fathers between the groups.

Table 5.1

Employed fathers

Category	Wing (n = 100)	Open school (n = 100)	Chi-square test	Level of significance
Intact families	29	36	$x^2 = 1.1168$, df = 1, $p > 0.10$	n.s.
Remarried fathers	6	4	$x^2 = 0.4211$, df = 1, $p > 0.10$	n.s.
Stepfathers	15	16	$x^2 = 2.1017$, df = 1, $p > 0.10$	n.s.
Single fathers	6	10	$x^2 = 0.611$, df = 1, $p > 0.18$	n.s.
TOTAL	56	66	$x^2 = 2.1017$, df = 1, $p > 0.10$	n.s.
Unknown occupations	44	34	$x^2 = 2.1017$, df = 1, $p > 0.10$	n.s.

Of the 'unknown occupations' little can be said save that it is improbable that their occupations differ markedly from those which are known. The occupations of the other 56 Wing fathers and 66 Open school fathers are discussed below.

It should be said that occupation and social class are highly correlated, but in a society of change, social class is not easily defined. High income sometimes rewards unskilled work and, in contrast, highly skilled professional work can be ill paid. Do money and social class correlate, as in American society? This problem permeates social assessment in our study in deciding which families have financial comfort and which are deprived economically. Some families live in luxurious surroundings, such as some fishermen and lorry drivers, while others in the same job scrape to survive. Yet fishermen are classed as Social Class IV (see below) and lorry drivers as Social Class III. Nurses are Social Class II but cannot be held as financially well off. Again, how are the unemployed classified, for they presumably will have the lowest standard of living? Single parents also, fathers and mothers, will be disadvantaged, yet good housekeeping and resourcefullness can compensate much. Only the social enquiry reports on the boys and the boys' own stories allow insight into the family.

Unemployment for fathers (natural and stepfathers)

Analysis found unemployment unexpectedly low (see Table 5.2) for figures for the intact families exclude the handicapped fathers on sick benefit (see Table 3.7).

Table 5.2

Unemployed fathers

Category		Wing (n = 100)		Open school (n = 100)	Chi-square test	Level of significance
Intact families	(55)	3	(50)	2	–	n.s.
Fathers remarrying	(6)	0	(5)	1	–	n.s.
Stepfathers	(15)	1	(16)	1*	–	n.s.
Single fathers	(6)	1**	(10)	2†		
TOTAL		5		6	$x^2 = 0.0962$, df = 1, $p > 0.10$	n.s.

Figures in parentheses relate to total numbers of families in each category.

*In prison for burglary

**In prison for wife murder

†Housekeepers for families of 5 and 6 children, wives having deserted.

The unemployed fathers came from areas of high unemployment, and their situation might be supposed to be due to the economic depression obtaining there, not to personal inadequacy. In some areas of Glasgow unemployment figures reach 36 per cent of males and in some families three generations of fathers have never worked.

The low incidence of fathers in prison is perhaps surprising, as was discussed earlier in this study. Their sons' incarceration is not, it appears, part of a general family pattern.

The two fathers who kept house for their families in the absence of the mother cannot be said to be truly 'unemployed' but rather fulfilling a necessary function for their numerous children.

Of the 11 'unemployed' fathers, 7 only can therefore be described as truly unemployed, prison and housekeeping being valid alternatives. Seven out of 200 is 3½ percent–lower than the national average for unemployment. Even if all 11 were counted the figure would be less than 6 per cent, i.e. the national average figure for Scotland in 1978.

Handicapped and unemployed fathers

The data are presented in Table 5.3. The point of emphasis is that the handicapped and unemployed fathers are not layabout ne'er-do-wells, but unfortunate men possibly suffering through no fault of their own. That their sons also suffer through the father's misfortune is an easily presumed corollary. The causes of their handicaps were discussed in Chapter 3.

Table 5.3

Handicapped and unemployed fathers

Category		Wing (n = 100)	Open school (n = 100)		Chi-square test	Level of significance
Intact families	(55)	23	(50)	12	$x^2 = 4.19$, df = 11, $0.05 > p > 0.02$	0.05
Fathers remarrying	(6)	0	(5)	0	–	n.s.
Stepfathers	(15)	1	(16)	0	–	n.s.
Single fathers	(6)	0	(10)	0	–	n.s.
TOTAL		24		12	$x^2 = 4.88$, df = 1, $0.05 > p > 0.02$	0.05

*Figures in parentheses relate to total numbers in each category

About half of the boys in both groups have broken families. Of the Wing boys who do have intact families (55) about half the number of their fathers are non-wage earning; and of the intact Open school families (5) about a quarter have non-wage earning fathers. In total, 68 per cent of the Wing fathers (45 lost and 23 handicapped) are non-contributing wage earners compared to 62 per cent in the Open school (50 lost fathers and 12 handicapped fathers).

These figures are higher than those found in Rushforth (1978): 'Nearly half of the boys have acute problems in relation to the male figure in their lives either on account of absence or his presentation of an inadequate or deviant role model' (p.26).

The present study is concerned with a group of 200 boys, half of whom are in high security. Rushforth's population was that of some 300 Scottish boys in senior and intermediate open schools. The difference found between the studies would result from the higher concentration of disadvantaged children in the high security unit, the Wing. Nevertheless, the figure for the disadvantaged Open school fathers is also higher.

Employment and unemployment in mothers

Employment in mothers in the normal population is increasing and is not now unusual as in past decades. The distinction between being 'unemployed' and being a 'housewife' is invidious in that the work of caring adequately for a numerous family is possibly harder than in any financially rewarded occupation having longer hours, no off duty and full responsibility. No staff in residential schools would tolerate such work. In our study the average size of family is five children with a range from 1 to 14 children. Handicapped fathers, 23 in the Wing and 12 in the Open school, are a further burden. It could not be said that such mothers are 'unemployed' if they care adequately for their husbands and families. Table 5.4 reveals the number of wage earning mothers overall.

Table 5.4

Wage earning mothers

Category		Wing (n = 100)		Open school (n = 100)	Chi-square test	Level of significance
Intact families	(55)	21	(50)	29	$x^2 = 1.7067$, df = 1 $p > 0.10$	n.s.
Handicapped families father non-wage earning	(23)	0	(12)	1	–	n.s.
Stepmothers	(6)	1	(5)	3	–	n.s.
Mothers remarrying	(15)	3	(10)	10	$x^2 = 4.0312$, df = 1, $0.05 > p > 0.01$	0.05
Single mothers	(17)	4	(17)	7	$x^2 = 0.8658$, df = 1, $p > 0.10$	n.s.
TOTAL		29		50	$x^2 = 9.2267$, df = 1, $0.01 > p > 0.001$	0.01

Figures in parentheses relate to the total numbers in each category

The Open school mothers are significantly higher than the Wing mothers in numbers as wage earners, the difference being somewhat influenced by the higher level of handicap in the Wing fathers. Only one mother is wage earning for both handicapped groups of fathers, 23 in the Wing and 12 in the Open school. If, therefore, maternal attendance in the home is significant in promoting family welfare, this finding is surprising for the Wing boys are, supposedly, more disturbed than the boys in the Open school.

The Open school working mothers also approximate more closely to the number of Open school working fathers than the Wing mothers (see Table 5.5) do to the Wing working fathers. Thus they appear more energetic and outgoing than the Wing mothers (see Table 5.6), even taking into account the handicap of the Wing fathers requiring attention at home.

Table 5.5

Wage earning parents in both groups compared

	Fathers	Mothers	Chi-square test	Level of significance
Wing	56	29	$x^2 = 14.9156$, df = 1, $0.001 > p$	Highly significant
Open school	66	50	$x^2 = 5.2544$, df = 1, $0.05 > p > 0.01$	0.05

Table 5.6

Comparison of mothers and fathers in terms of employment (both groups)

	Wing	Open school	Chi-square test	Level of significance
Mothers	29	50	$x^2 = 9.2269$, df = 1, $0.01 > p > 0.001$	0.01
Fathers	56	66	$x^2 = 2.1017$, df = 1, $p > 0.10$	n.s.

It is of interest to note that although a significant difference exists between maternal wage earning in the groups, there is no difference for paternal employment.

Fathers' occupations and social class

It seems relevant to quote from the Registrar General's 'Classification of Occupations' as construed by Nisbet and Entwistle (1970) as a guide to the social class of the families of the boys now studied. The Registrar General's scale is as follows:

I Professional and managerial occupations

II Intermediate occupations

III Skilled occupations

IV Partly skilled occupations

V Unskilled occupations

'Social class III', observe Nisbet and Entwistle, 'is the largest section of the population and does not distinguish between certain non-manual and clerical occupations and manual occupations.' They recommend grouping I and II together and dividing Social Class III into manual and non-manual skilled workers as follows:

I/II Professional and Managerial

Accountants, actuaries, accountings, costing, pay and bank clerks, architects, army, navy and air force officers, civil servants (administrative and executive grade), officers of local authorities, clergymen, doctors, engineers (with degree qualifications), farmers, lawyers, managers, nurses, pharmacists, police inspectors, shop proprietors and managers, surveyors, teachers.

III Non-manual: clerical and non-manual skilled

Clerks (including civil service and local government clerical grades), assistant nurses, medical auxiliaries, commercial travellers, hairdressers, policemen, post office sorters, telegraphists and supervisors, secretaries (not company secretaries), shorthand typists and office machine operators, shop assistants.

III Manual: skilled manual

Builders, masons, plasterers, slaters, carpenters, joiners, plumbers, painters, electricians, fitters, mechanics, machine erectors, radio mechanics, platers, riveters, metal workers, instrument makers, bus and lorry drivers, roundsmen and van drivers, printers, engine drivers, skilled railway workers, skilled agricultural workers, tailors, H.M. Forces (other ranks), trawler skippers.

IV Semi-skilled

Agricultural labourers, labourers, barmen, bus conductors, foundry labourers, garment machinists, laundry workers, packers, oilers and greasers, railway firemen, fishermen.

V Unskilled

Dock labourers, navvies, porters, lift attendants, costermongers, hawkers, newspaper sellers, watchmen, kitchen hands.

In our cohort there are no children who obviously come from Class I and few from Class II. Rich families and families with connections which enable their deviant children to be handled privately are not represented. Morris and McIzaac (1978) discuss this as it concerns our Scottish Hearings system. Martin and Murray (1976) should also be consulted. Finlayson (1976) writes: 'In cases where the Reporter believes that the parents can cope with the situation he will take no action'. Apparently Social Classes I and II are outside the scope of our children in compulsory residential care. Parsloe (1978) holds the same view.

The massive body of modern sociocriminological literature now appearing in both Britain and America is pointing towards the idea that the deprived, male, urban and young are punished. Others of privileged groups are 'treated' by parents and professionals and if all fails these children go to expensive private schools (Lambert and Millham, 1968) where high fees allow the parents to shift the training of their unruly children to school masters who have an 'understanding' with the law. The Matthew Effect (Burstall, 1977) hits out again.

Taylor, Walton and Young (1973 and 1975) review the literature, both seminal and recent, British, European and American, on the theme of social deviance. Paul Wiles (1971 and 1975) reviews the fundamental, and at times radical, re-examination of criminological theorising which has been undertaken in Britain over the last few years. Farrington and West are continuing to carry out an impressive programme of research in the Cambridge Institute of Criminology, funded by the Home Office. Two major university centres of teaching and research have also been set up: one by Radzinowicz at Cambridge and another by Mannheim at the London School of Economics. Paul Wiles himself works in the Centre for Criminological Studies in Sheffield. Parsloe's important study of juvenile justice in Britain and America is further essential reading.

It is apparent that the study of delinquency has broadened from the Victorian view of it as 'sin' into considering it as an interesting aspect of civil and social life. Our present study is concerned with analysis of our two groups and their antecedents. The fascinating study of the literature cannot detain us here but it is the background against which the boys should be viewed. Treatment similar to that of the privileged children of Social Classes I and II may eventually percolate downwards when children of other classes offend society.

Examination of fathers' jobs in both groups, using the Registrar General's broad outlines of social class, finds the greater number are Social Class III, skilled manual workers. This is the same situation in the

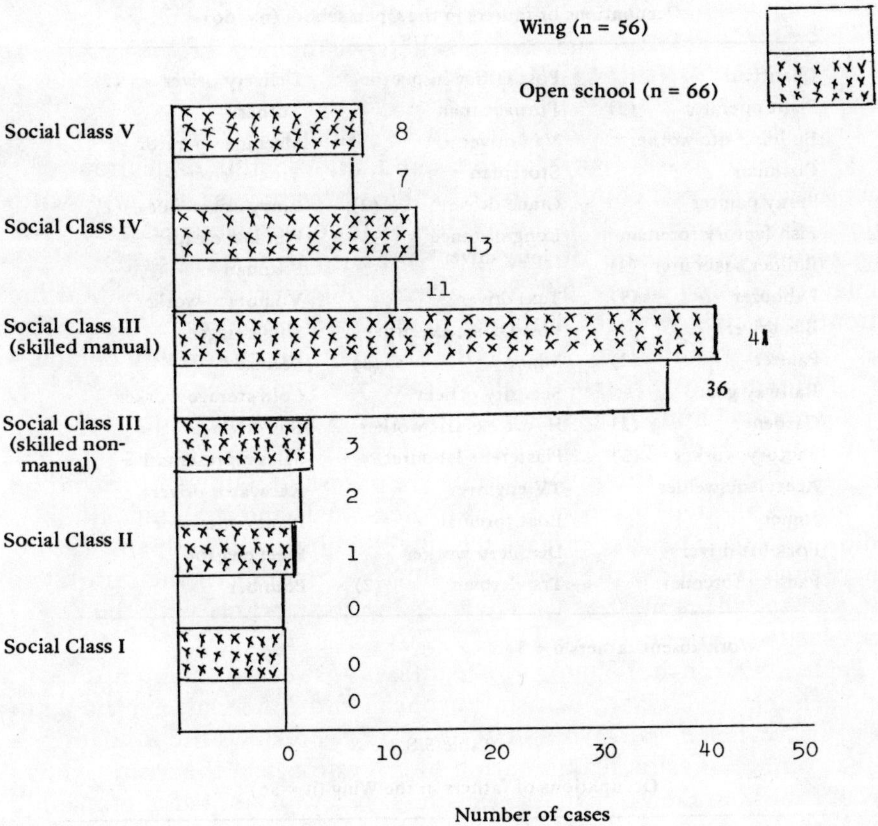

Figure 5.1 Social class by fathers' jobs

Wing fathers (n = 56)	0	0	2	36	11	7
Open school fathers (n = 66)	0	1	3	41	13	8
	Social Class I	Social Class II	Social Class III (skilled non-manual)	Social Class III (skilled manual)	Social Class IV	Social Class V

Table 5.7

Occupations of fathers in the Open school (n = 66)

Chauffeur		Post Office inspector		Delivery driver	(2)
Plant operator	(2)	Furnace man		Turner	
Building site worker		Van driver		Machine operator	
Coalman		Storeman		Truck driver	
Spray painter		Crane driver	(2)	Lorry driver (local)	(2)
Fish factory foreman		Long distance lorry driver *		Window cleaner	
Builder's labourer	(2)			Postman	
Labourer	(3)	Taxi driver		Voluntary worker	
Bus driver		Post Office executive		Ship's rigger	
Painter	(2)	Miner	(3)	Seaman *	
Railway guard		Security officer		Cold storage worker	
Gardener	(3)	Hydro electric worker		Bus driver	
Factory worker	(3)	Plasterer's labourer		Sales representative	
Acetylene welder		TV engineer		Excavator driver	
Joiner		Boat foreman		Plant contractor	
Fork-lift driver		Distillery worker		Steel erector	
Factory foreman		Trawlerman	(2)	Plumber	

*Work absent fathers n = 3

Table 5.8

Occupations of fathers in the Wing (n = 56)

Soldier		Baker		Dunlop tyre worker	
Plumber	(2)	Crane driver		Sanitary worker	(2)
Steel erector		Car worker	(2)	Linwood truck driver	
Steel worker	(2)	Railway track worker		Labourer	(3)
Car worker (self employed)		Textile worker		Merchant seaman *	
Fish filleter		Sawmill worker		Plasterer's labourer	
Fisherman	(2)	Factory worker	(2)	Fork-lift driver	
Skilled plastic worker		Tinker	(4)	Insulation engineer	
Plastic worker		Butcher	(2)	Goods truck driver	(2)
Driver		Electrician			
Salesman *		Shot blaster		Joiner	
Coal merchant		Painter	(2)	Bricklayer	
Blaster in furnace		Building worker		Cement fixer	
Motor mechanic		Spinner		Bus driver	

*Work absent fathers n = 4

general population as observed by Nisbet and Entwistle. Precise allocation of occupation to class is impossible because all jobs are not in the Registrar General's classification. Figure 5.1 gives a general picture and Tables 5.7 and 5.8 show particular jobs. Given that there are 66 known jobs in the Open school to the 56 in the Wing, the spread of social class appears much the same in both groups.

No case appears in either group in Social Class I but one Open school father, a 'Post Office Inspector' is in Social Class II. In Social Class III (skilled non-manual) only three cases occur in the Open school and one in the Wing. The Wing father is a travelling salesman and the Open school fathers are two Post Office workers and one travelling salesman.

Social Class III (skilled manual) unexpectedly does not contain many work absent fathers in either group, such as lorry drivers, train guards or seamen. Social Class III (skilled manual) contains the main group of fathers for both groups.

Social Class IV has no significant differences in number or type of jobs between the groups.

In Social Class V, four fathers in the Wing cohort are 'scrap merchants'. This is a euphemism for tinkers, hawkers and 'travelling people'. The boys from these families relate that 'money is never short'. Any rubbish dump wherever provides valuable 'pickings' for the skilled 'gatherer' in scrap metal and other materials. In 'Womble' country there is abundance. By contrast, there are no 'tinkers' in the Open school. This is interesting, four as compared to none. The probability is that sons of 'travelling people' find it difficult to accept placement in List D schools in confinement and abscond so frequently that they eventually land in secure accommodation. The initial placement in List D would derive from theft, endemic in scrap merchants and tinkers, for the demarcation line between theft and 'taking' is ill defined. Copper piping, lead, any valuable scrap is always a temptation in unguarded situations to the opportunist 'travelling people'.

Whether tinkers are Social Class V or not is questionable in that money, the boys say, is not short and living is easy. The life of builder's labourer, navvy and kitchen hand must be much less acceptable.

Mothers' occupations and social class

Figure 5.2 shows that Open school and Wing mothers parallel each other closely in occupations and social class, allowing for the difference in numbers in the groups–Wing (29) and Open school (50). The same mirroring was observed in the fathers' social class. Figure 5.2 and Tables 5.9 and 5.10 show the mothers' particular jobs.

However, fathers' occupations cluster in Social Class III (skilled manual)

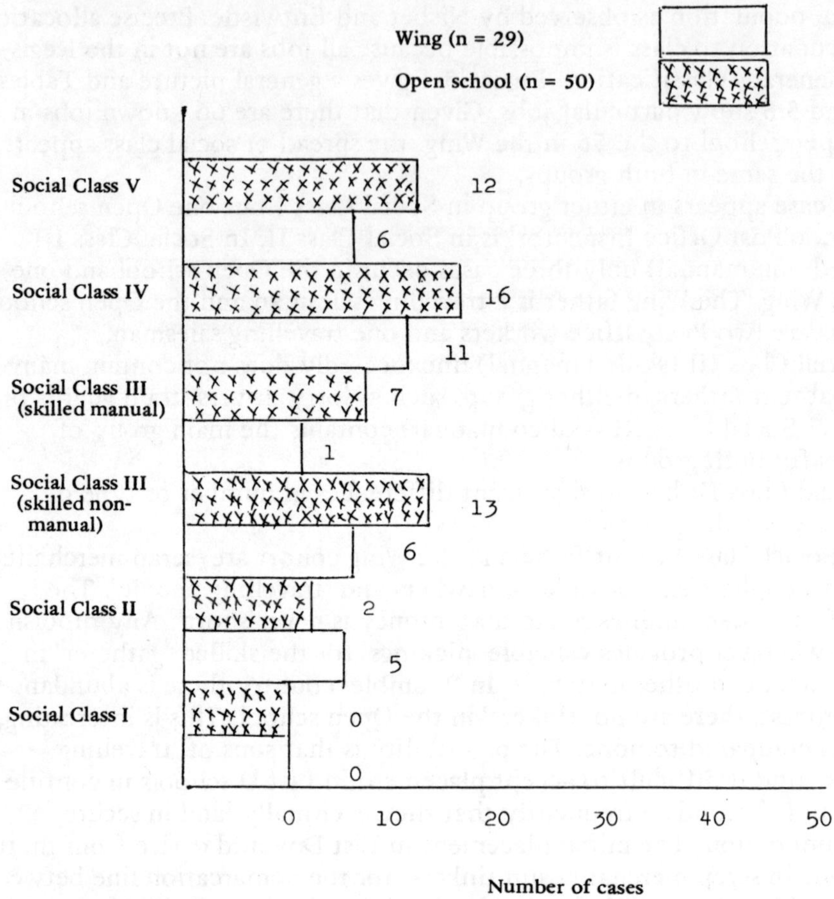

	Social Class I	Social Class II	Social Class III (skilled non-manual)	Social Class III (skilled manual)	Social Class IV	Social Class V
Wing mothers (n = 29)	0	5	6	1	11	6
Open school mothers (n = 50)	0	2	13	7	16	12

Figure 5.2 Social class by mothers' jobs

Table 5.9

Occupations of mothers in the Wing (n = 29)

Cleaner	(3)	Waitress	(2)	Fish filleter	
Home help		Nursing sister	(2)	Railway cleaner	
Tinker		Hosiery worker		Bus conductress	
Shop assistant	(3)	Factory worker	(3)	Manageress in large store	
Hospital orderly		Clerk		Part time cleaner	
Geriatric nurse		Threadmill worker		Hotel worker	
Nurse	(2)	Sales representative		Switchboard operator	

Table 5.10

Occupations of mothers in the Open school (n = 50)

Shorthand typist		School meals helper	(2)	Cook in factory	(2)
Hospital cleaner		Instructor in factory		Net worker	
Buffet manageress		Factory worker		Cleaner	(5)
Part time cleaner	(2)	Shop assistant	(5)	Auxiliary nurse	(3)
Taxi driver		Bus cleaner		Factory cleaner	
Car cleaner		Barmaid		Factory canteen worker	
Garage cleaner		Hospital cleaner	(2)	Domestic help	
Hotel worker	(2)	Bus conductress		Qualified pharmacist	
Canteen helper		Psychiatric nursing sister		School cleaner	(3)
Fish worker	(2)	Hospital aid		Hospital worker	

whereas mothers are spread through Social Class III, IV and V. These two latter groupings occur because mothers without training are able to take only 'unskilled' jobs as cleaners in schools, factories, garages and hospitals, as casual workers, when family duties allow. Few are Social Class III (skilled manual) where the bulk of fathers lie.

It is interesting, however, that mothers occur more frequently than fathers in Social Class III (skilled non-manual), as typists, switchboard operators, sales representatives and shop assistants.
In Social Class II there are, according to the Registrar General's categories, seven women, five from the Wing and two from the Open school. (There is only one father in this group, the Post Office inspector.) These mothers are five nurses (two are nursing sisters), one a qualified pharmacist and one a manageress of a large fashion business.

Summary and conclusion

About half the families in both groups are non-intact, 45 in the Wing and 50 in the Open school. Of those that are whole more than half in the Wing have fathers handicapped by accident or illness who are not wage earning. In the Open school about one quarter of the intact families are similarly handicapped. Thus around three quarters of the total cohort of 200 boys have disadvantaged families, with non-wage contributing natural fathers, higher than was found in the Rushforth study, which was dealing with a population in open schools and not focussing on the high security unit and its sister open school.

Information on the occupations of fathers is not complete in that 39 per cent of fathers in the cohort of 200 have disappeared (i.e. 78 fathers). It is, however, unlikely that their jobs will differ much from those which are known.

Examination of jobs according to the Registrar General's classification reveals that the existing fathers of the boys in both groups come mainly from the skilled manual Social Class III group of the population; and that working mothers range more widely throughout the social classes excepting Social Class I and minimally in Social Class II.

Mothers have a much higher level of wage earning employment in the Open school group than the Wing mothers and, conversely, mothers in the Wing are significantly higher in number as housewives.

Unemployment in both groups is low in fathers (or father figures) who are physically fit.

Highly educated, rich and influential parents are not represented in the cohort.

6 Geographical distribution of cases

The large Scottish cities provide the majority of cases, boys' homes being in the areas of deprivation and unemployment where leisure opportunities for non-delinquent activities are few for the young (see Table 6.1).

Table 6.1
Geographical distribution of cases

Region	Total number of boys in Forest	Wing	Open school	Chi-square test	Level of significance
Strathclyde	97	63	34	$x^2 = 15.69$, df = 1, $0.001 > p$	0.001
Tayside	31	7	24	$x^2 = 9.77$, df = 1, $0.001 > p$	0.001
Lothian	27	12	15	$x^2 = 0.17$, df - 1, $p > 0.10$	n.s.
Grampian	15	7	8	–	–
Fife	13	4	9	–	n.s.
Highland	9	3	6	–	–
Central	5	1	4	–	–
Dumfries and Galloway	3	3	0	–	–
Borders	0	0	0	–	–
Islands	0	0	0	–	–
TOTAL	200	100	100		

Strathclyde

Strathclyde provides 97 cases from the total cohort of 200 in this study. It has Glasgow as its centre and numerous outlying towns. Half of the Scottish population lives in this region so the numbers are proportionate.

At one time a prosperous area with shipbuilding and heavy industry, Strathclyde is now in decline, with unemployment at the highest level in

Britain and a falling population. Some citizens have never been employed. Its slums are said to be the worst in Europe, with decaying tenements and many areas devastated for rebuilding which is slow to begin. On the outskirts of the city immense housing estates without social facilities were built after the war, dormitory suburbs without shops, pubs or parks. Boredom leads to vandalism and the facilities which existed in some areas now look as if impaired by warfare. In Pollock, for example, burned houses flank houses with broken windows, though here and there is the exceptional house with curtains and even flowering window boxes. Margot MacDonald, ex-Scottish Nationalist MP, mourns the lot of the 'wasted lives' of the people who dwell there. High rise flats are a further aspect of Glasgow life in which families are rehoused from derelict tenements and have lost what play areas there were for children—'jungles with windows'. By contrast, a magnificent motorway strides through the centre of Glasgow, towering over the broken down houses lying below.

Nevertheless, Glasgow has some splendid buildings and some areas are very beautiful. Differences between rich and poor are very marked and lie close together. The Glasgow character, too, is engaging and sympathetic. Wit and laughter are endemic in all its citizens. Sudden comic turns of phrase are normal as the answer a town councillor made to a questioner who asked why the lower windows of the housing department were made of reinforced glass. 'We need it against bullets.'

The Strathclyde area has ten List D schools of its own but still takes up places in Forest. In our study 34 cases are in the Open school and 63 in the Wing. Thus one third of the Open school boys are from Strathclyde and about two thirds in the Wing, the latter a distillation of 'difficult' boys said to be 'uncontainable' in other schools and funnelled to high security placement. Until 1976 the Wing was the only secure unit in Scotland but with the opening of the Merchant Wing in Glasgow the numbers from there should diminish. When a further secure unit (now being built) is also opened, numbers should be fewer still unless the children at present on long term placing in penal establishments can be diverted to this accommodation, as is expected.

Table 6.1 shows that the proportion of boys in the Wing, in all other regions save Strathclyde, is less than in the Open school. But 63 per cent of the Wing boys come from Strathclyde, geographically distant from their homes, and they are thus exiled from parental contact. Even on leaves home the journey is both daunting and expensive. The Wing perhaps is the more comforting as so many boys have been neighbours at home in Strathclyde—an island of western boys in Forest.

The Strathclyde boys

Examination of the home areas of the boys in Strathclyde shows a widely scattered distribution. No one district dominates as a source and the characteristics of districts are not constant over periods of time. For example, Easterhouse—notorious for gang warfare and delinquency a decade ago—has only one boy in the Wing, probably reflecting improved social amenities. The Gorbals, equally celebrated at one period, also has only one case, now being largely demolished by town planners and the population rehoused elsewhere. Bleak housing estates on the outskirts of the town feature more largely. Drumchapel, Ruchazie, Castlemilk, Possilpark, Pollock, Carntyne and Springburn are the addresses of about four boys each. Outlying towns like Irvine, Hamilton, Johnstone, Kilwinning, Kilmarnock, Ayr, Motherwell and Coatbridge give a quota of one to four boys each. Unemployment is high in these areas and social amenities low. Irvine has recently opened a fine sports centre which may lower the social misdemeanours of its youngsters.

Paisley, with a concentration of poor housing in Ferguslie Park on its outskirts, has five boys in the Wing from a geographical area of about one square mile. Two of these boys, released to return home and to normal school, returned to the Wing a few months later, glad to be back again, deteriorated, thin, neglected, truant and dirty. Ferguslie Park is an area which is difficult to believe exists in the late 1970s. Many houses are fire-damaged and empty; others are boarded up, the refuge of truant children or homeless folk. Houses which are inhabited are unpainted and run down. Packs of semi-wild dogs roam the area, breeding indiscriminately and increasing steadily, surviving on house waste. Few cars are visible outside the houses. A shopping centre in the middle of the estate is armoured with metal shutters and closed. An off licence was the sole surviving shop when last I visited Ferguslie Park in September 1977.

Paisley's centre is beautiful, reflecting the former wealth of the cotton trade. Gardens, fountains and fine architecture embellish it. It appears a world apart from the wretched area described above which sends five of its children from a small group of deprived families to a high security unit.

In Glasgow the difficulties of the social work department are great and no one could envy its task in attempting to aid its citizens in need. Yet, for all the problems, the boys in Forest overall are not proportionally over-represented in terms of Strathclyde's population which is half that of Scotland.

The letter reproduced here gives a window into this world. It is from an absconder from Forest to a friend still in the Wing. It reveals vividly the thinking of the teenager in a Strathclyde culture pattern of high delinquency and low socioeconomic status in an urban area where gang warfare is endemic. The pathos of its pretentious claim to sex and violence is disturbing. The boy himself is young, slightly built, fresh faced, blushing easily and not intelligent—a fledgling. The child's nickname was Bulb because he coloured up so easily.

Dear D-J

Just a few lines to let you no that I am
getting on fine. Well D-J I cant wait till you gett
out because we are having a great time because last
week we were fighting Down the glen, a couple
well not a couple about 17 guys chased us with
hatches and knifes. Well D-J on thursday June
went up to louisa and me and ma mate went up
to his big brothers and when we were comeing back
Down the hill we saw five guys getting into
June and we ran Down ma mate grabed one and
Stuck a big knife in him, a grabed one smasht
a bottle or his head and then stuck it in
his face, well D-J the polis are looking for
us, well D-J every time we see the polis we
have to run, well D-J we are having a great
time. Well D-J carol fell out wa me but she
wants to go back wa me but D-J as you no I run
after no bird but at the same time I am getting
off with alot of birds Well D-J I have nothing
eles to say so I will have to close for now
So goodbye for now

D-J

Nevertheless, all children in deprived areas are not delinquent. One boy indignantly defended his home area: 'There are good folk in Drumchapel!' Perhaps, however, it is more difficult for children to be 'good' there.

Figure 6.1 Advertisement for social workers in Drumchapel. This advertisement ran in a social work magazine in 1978. It speaks volumes.

Reproduced with the permission of Strathclyde Social Work Department and *Community Care*.

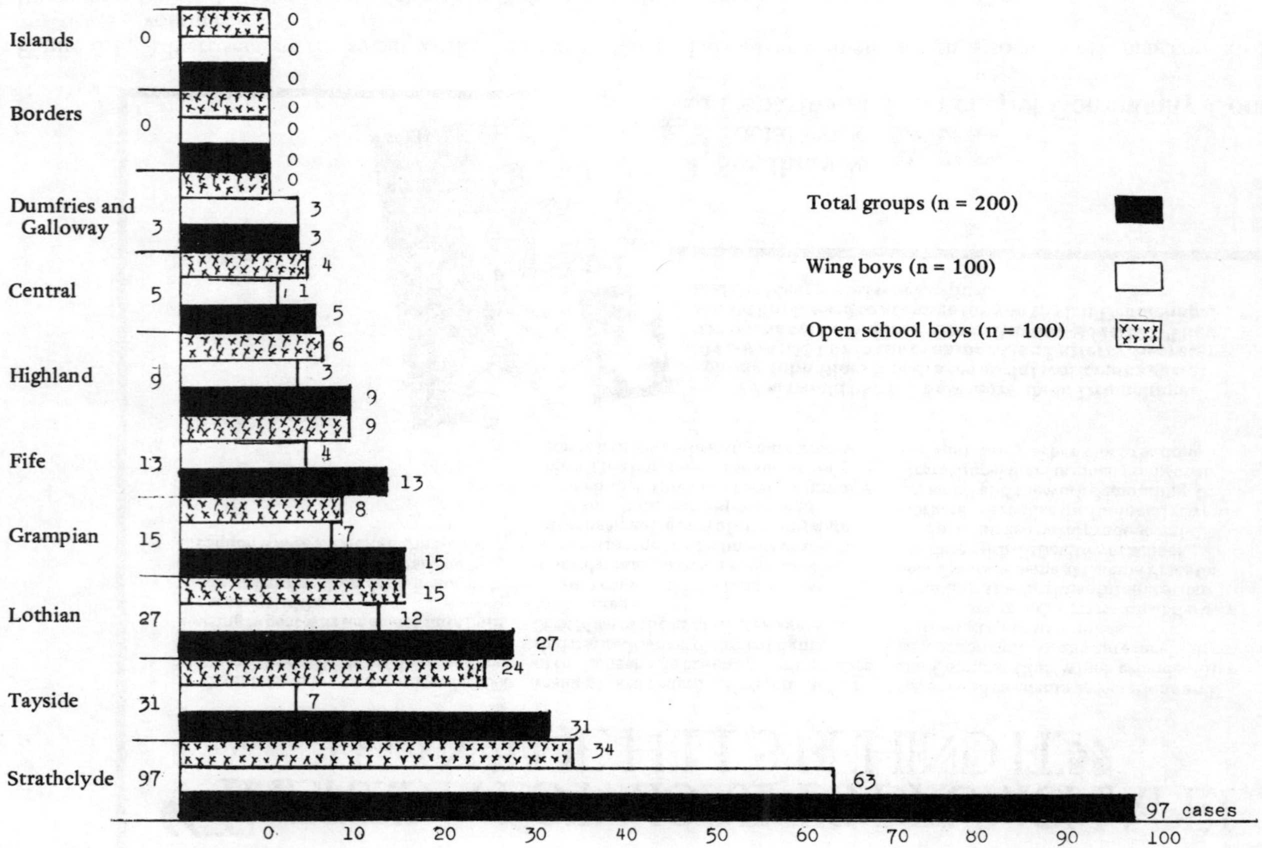

Figure 6.2 Geographical origin of boys

Other regions

Table 6.1 and Figure 6.2 show that Tayside and Lothian, Central, Grampian and Highland regions follow Strathclyde in the numbers of boys they send to Forest. Edinburgh, Dundee and Perth, Aberdeen, Stirling and Inverness are Scotland's main cities so these rates would be expected in ratio of population. Each city has its own areas of deprivation, of low socioeconomic level, and it is from there that the boys derive. Aberdeen, for instance, has one small area, in merely one block of streets, from which four boys have come.

Outside the cities the country areas have few boys in compulsory residential care. Regions without large towns, such as the Borders and Islands, have no children in Forest. It would seem that, where the population is not concentrated in deprived areas in towns, children are less difficult or else adults are more patient and use community resources for their upbringing.

Martin and Murray (1976) warn against 'interpreting figures as the true measures of the levels of delinquency prevailing in different parts of the country', as many variables are in operation, e.g. police policy, reporters' policy, the policy of Courts and the views of the social work departments. Yet it is consistently true that the children in this study come from the towns and from certain areas there. This is especially noticeable in Strathclyde where its rural areas yield few or no children.

Parsloe (1978) writes, 'children subjected to processing by the law are not randomly selected. They come from the poorer and more disadvantaged groups in society, whose values and behavioural patterns may run counter to those of the prevailing middle class establishment. In addition, they suffer from *powerlessness* and do not have access to the methods of rebutting deviant labelling which better educated, better housed and more adequately financed families usually have'. Such children in the compulsory residential system come, as seen above, from clearly observed geographical areas.

Summary

Strathclyde, with half the population of Scotland, has nearly one half of the total Forest population of 200 boys. The level of Strathclyde boys in the Wing is significantly higher than in the Open school, comprising two thirds of the population there.

Boys are from urban and deprived areas and rarely from country districts. When population is not concentrated, children tend to be cared for in their own community.

No non-Caucasian boys were in the cohort of the 200 boys studied.

7 The boys themselves

The study so far has been concerned with the sources of sentencing, the offences of the boys, their families, their previous placements, their geographical origin and the employment and social class of parents. The focus is now concentrated on the boys themselves.

Age

The boys in the Open school are fourteen and a half years of age and upwards on entry. However, some boys may stay on in school until they are well past their sixteenth birthday—even to seventeen plus years. The date of their first psychological interview with the writer was used as one point of time from which to calculate ages. Figure 7.1 and Table 7.1 show that most boys are between fifteen and a half to sixteen years. The school likes to release boys at Christmas or in early June near the sixteenth birthday when a normal school leaving date occurs and employment becomes possible. Nevertheless, some boys—particularly the Section 206(2) boys—may stay longer until the Parole Board meets and considers it wise for them to return home.

Figure 7.1 shows that although the Open school boys are closely grouped from age fifteen to sixteen and a half the Wing boys are not so closely clustered. One boy is only twelve and a half and, at the other extreme, one is seventeen and a half. The numbers of Wing boys rise slowly from the youngest to the same peak numbers as the Open school boys at fifteen and a half.

The Open school boys are therefore homogeneous in ages from fifteen years to sixteen and a half, whereas the Wing boys are widely spread. This means that the Wing has to shelter boys from twelve and a half to seventeen and a half and, as in a family where younger brothers live with older brothers, each influenced by the other and subject to the same regime of care. Naturally the age difference gives the older boys considerable status *vis-à-vis* the younger, and the potential for bullying is closely guarded against by the staff.

Relationships with staff and other boys

The population of the Wing is usually around 20 boys, ranging from 16

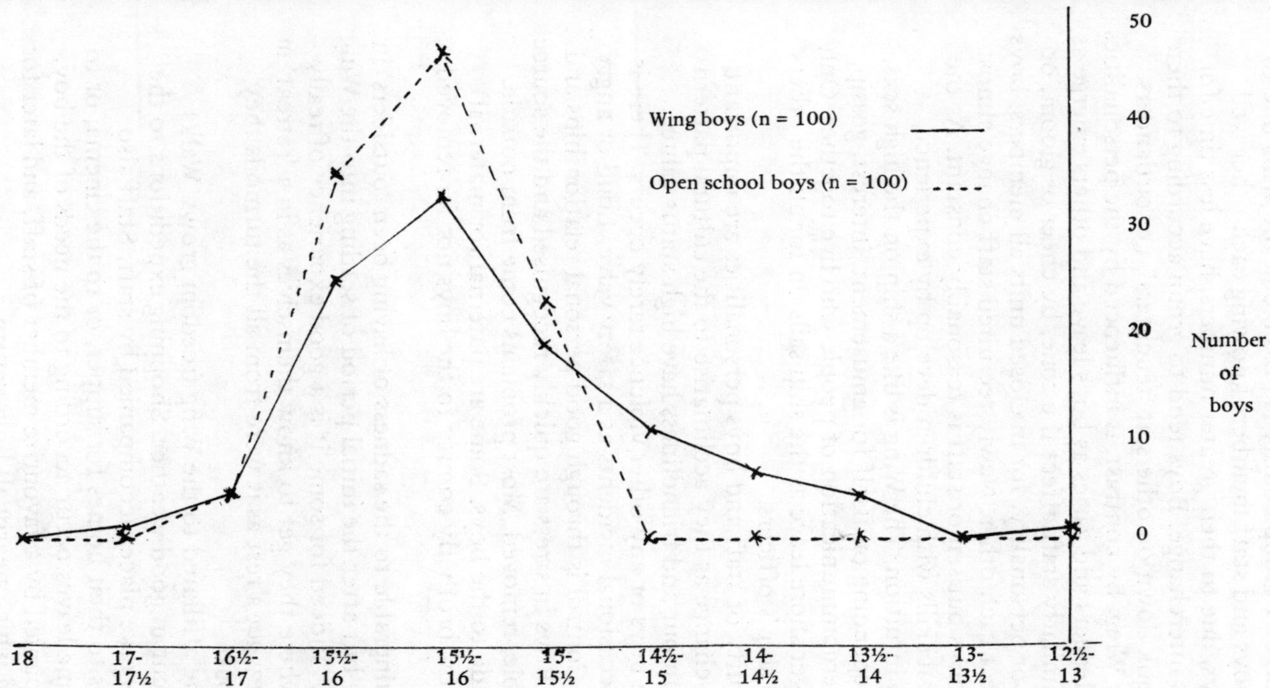

Figure 7.1 Ages of boys at first interview

Table 7.1
Ages of boys at first interview

Age	12½	13	13½	14	14½	15	15½	16	16½	17
Wing boys (n = 100)	1	0	4	6	10	18	32	24	4	1
Open school boys (n = 100)	0	0	0	0	0	22	45	29	4	0

to 25. The Open school has greater numbers, 60 to 90, according to seasonal variations. Greater group comity is possible in the Wing due to the small numbers, boys and staff members knowing each other well. The Open school boys, due to their greater numbers, have less time for staff contact and less interchange. Boys tend to group according to their place of origin and look down on others at 'teuchters', i.e. outlanders.

The climate of the Wing, by contrast, is influenced by the personalities of the boys who are leaders and varies as boys leave and others emerge as having high status. Similarly staff affect the tone, by cheer or gloom, or any variant of mood or personality, for in closed units all members, boys and staff, closely affect each other. Newly recruited staff change almost as frequently as the boys but senior staff is reasonably constant. As the years pass their natural skills with children develop by experience, training and sensitive intuition. The Wing is like a ship on the high seas, isolated from land, depending on itself for amusement, interest, gossip, gloom and all the intercommunication of people who live together. Only boys nearing release get shore leave as the ship sails on for all the others under its skipper and ship's officers.

In the close contiguity of staff and boys personalities are important and in some measure change as they acclimatise to the cultural pattern of the Wing. Good humour and friendliness have high status value. Fighting between the boys or any other violence rarely occurs. There is no swearing save in occasional incidents as a safety valve. Loud or angry voices are not heard. Control is through good personal relationships and the security of calm. Boys in stress are quickly recognised and the source assessed and, if possible, removed. Most problems come from outside.

Staff vary in attitude to the boys. Some are paternal (or maternal). Younger members show brotherly comity to the boys not far removed from them in age.

All the boys are vulnerable to the sadness of having been 'outsiders' in their previous history but after the initial period of settling into the Wing they are not unhappy. Indeed for some it is a good experience of really being cared for and where they get to know themselves as in a 'retreat' in a monastic order. They get a rest as it were from all the turmoils they have survived in the past.

As the boys become affiliated to the Wing freedom grows. Walks around the school occur in good weather. Shopping expeditions to the local town sometimes take place, accompanied by staff. Staff also frequently invite boys to their homes for supper, or to the cinema, or to football matches. Home leaves occur according to the needs of the boy, first for a day accompanied by a favourite member of staff, and later for week long leaves from which nearly all boys return.

There is undoubtedly much goodwill between staff and boys and such staff who do not fit into this ambience quickly disappear to find other employment. Cawson (1978) in her study of residential staff found that in the English system most staff were young and without training and rarely stayed longer than two years in post. This is not entirely true of the Wing, for although there is considerable movement there is also continuity.

The situation in the Wing is constantly evolving, and the administration is flexible. Decisions are taken communally by the staff after discussion. A continual dilemma the staff endure is the position concerning security. The public are not sympathetic to absconders. The staff therefore hold the balance between the guilt they feel in keeping the boys and the need to take them out. Millham et al (1978) writes that boys in secure accommodation have many more treats and outside expeditions for this reason than boys in 'open' schools.

It is not suggested that boys would choose to come to the Wing and remain there. But most will take away good memories and remember well the people with whom they grew to be friends. Nor is it suggested that conditions could not be improved, nor that the climate is always 'coming up roses'. Boys do fall out with each other; staff fall out with each other too, as in any society. But by and large there is much to commend.

A former headmaster described the Wing as a potential 'time bomb', quoting disturbances in the first few years after its opening. At that time little was known about closed units. The original organisation was highly regimented. Boys wore short trousers and shirts with rolled up sleeves. Staff were ordered not to be over-friendly, believing that friendliness would be damaging to good order. Boys marched briskly to sharp commands. They were locked in their quarters much of the day. Eventually these conditions resulted in a widely publicised disturbance, in which two members of staff were severely injured in a breakdown of order, and boys appeared before the Sheriff charged with serious assault.

Subsequent to this episode money was poured into the Wing; salaries were raised with a consequent improvement in the calibre of staff. It was clearly seen that 'opening up' was necessary for a closed unit. Since then, over fifteen years ago, skills have accrued in working with the boys by good personal relationships, mutual respect and esteem. Sensitivity to atmosphere, the picking up of cues given almost subliminally, and a concerned and familial watchfulness contribute to this care. It is a masculine regime (although there are women on the staff) that the boys themselves understand. Indeed most of the Wing boys, as we have seen, have not hitherto experienced stability and calm, and they do develop gradually in maturity, modelling themselves on the behaviour of the staff as children do in the normal school on the behaviour of their teachers.

The boys learn to be themselves, not fugitives from society, as they have been in the past, 'living rough', self-selected Ishmaels, hungry, thieving, unsheltered and prey to opportunists. They are in the Wing in a time of peace.

Adolescence in children in the normal community has traditionally been viewed as a time of stress as the child develops through pubescence to adulthood. Body size increases rapidly, sexual characteristics emerge, dependence on adults decreases. Rutter's study (1970) of the child population in the Isle of Wight found ten per cent of the child population maladjusted, a view well supported by other writers. Coleman (1974) however believes that adolescence 'far from being a period of storm and stress is, for the most of young people, a time of relative stability'. The myth of the wild, disturbed adolescent is for him a 'paper tiger'. Boys in compulsory residential establishments, and more so in high security units, in their patient and genial behaviour incline the present writer to Coleman's view.

Indeed if these boys are the 'worst' boys in Scotland the general picture must be very good. They are courteous, friendly, and gentle, nor in the four years spent as a psychologist in the school have I seen a boy of whom I could not approve eventually.

It is of course due to the skills of the staff that the climate is so mellow among the boys. There is no 'brain washing'. But there is care and concern, sometimes exercised also towards the staff by the boys themselves. Sadly, nevertheless, as the following chapter will show, 'trouble' lies ahead in plenty for most of the boys after release.

The Open school boys, all much the same age, do not have this diversity of age and are less dependent on each other and staff. They move around the school with their instructors and interest focusses on weekend leaves and holidays. Their main wish and talk concerns release. Absconding varies with weather, and mood, and often there are periods with none (Clarke and Martin 1971, Millham, Bullock and Hosie 1978).

Assessment

Each of the 200 boys was assessed by the writer in psychological interviews and became well known over the period of time spent in the school. This varied from about ten months up to two years. All Hearing boys must be reviewed within a year (although they can seek a review on their own initiative at three or six months) and are usually released at the Review Hearing. Section 413 cases also spend about one year in the school irrespective as to whether they were sentenced for one or two years as release is in the remit of the Secretary of State through his officials. Section 206(2) cases may spend a longer time due to the many hurdles involved by the procedure of parole. These months therefore allow many contacts with the psychologist and frequent interviews and consultations occur. Review meetings, case conferences and private conversations also allow the view of staff on the boy to be gathered. The boys' field social workers are also consulted when they visit their boys in the Wing. Home visits sometimes occur and parents are seen in the Wing whenever possible.

Interviews with the boys are individual initially but group sessions also occur later. Informal meetings at meals, in class, on walks and at games also take place.

The Wing boys are known to the writer in greater depth than the Open school boys in that they are fewer, around 20 in number at any one time, so more frequent contacts are possible; and in the hour at lunch in the Wing the boys gather around to talk and be social. Thus each week (the psychologist spends two days each week in Forest) the Wing boys are seen, some individually and others in the social group, and depth of knowledge grows. This is not physically possible in the Open school where the numbers fluctuate from 60 to 90. Grouping is larger and more formal there. Frequent individual interviews which allow depth therapy to develop must necessarily be infrequent due to the numbers and the time needed for assessment of new cases. Melanie Klein (1932) in private psychotherapy of children noted 'some improvement after the four hundred and eighty-third interview'. Such frequency is not even dreamed of in the List D setting, however much it might be desired.

The skills needed in the psychologist which allow boys to accept a psychological interview and to respond in a natural and unrestrained manner grow only with experience, intuition and good fortune. Boys come to the compulsory residential setting with tight reservations about psychologists for there is a latent fear that an interview may be prodromal to removal to mental hospital. Jokes hostile to the psychologists are part of the culture of most institutions, self-protective because of this anxiety. Nevertheless, in the cohort studied the boys lost this sentiment in that all the boys were seen without distinction and it is hoped that no 'bad' results eventuated for any boy. Indeed it may even be said that boys sought, and seek, interviews, offended if neglected. The personal relationship and interview is valued. 'When can I see you?' is the continual question. In the interview their talk is of home, of their town, their girl, their feelings of loneliness and the respite, especially in the Wing, from heavy stresses 'outside'. In an institution predominantly male in staff, women are cherished. The boys are friendly, beyond flattery, displacing to some extent the affection they feel for mothers and grandmothers and their extended family onto the women of the staff. When this climate of opinion includes the psychologist, interviews are rewarding and the outcomes valid, in that the boy has the total attention of the adult to whom he is talking. He is himself and not in a group, in a one-to-one relation. Privacy is rare in an institution and correspondingly valued even in so small a group as the Wing.

It is important before seeing a boy to read his file thoroughly. In the file are the accounts given by social workers (for he may have had more than one), psychiatric reports, psychological reports, assessment centre reports and school reports, or reports from Longriggend—a rag bag of opinions on the child. The file varies in size from a few pages to a volume, depending on the boy's history.

It is disturbing that few psychological and psychiatric reports are found in the boys' files. It could be supposed that in the assessments made on the fates of offending children advice would be sought from both sources. Yet the number of such reports for both groups is as shown in Table 7.2.

Table 7.2

Psychological and psychiatric reports

	Psychological report	Psychiatric report	Chi-square test	Level of significance
Wing boys (n = 100)	13	24	$x^2 = 3.32$, df = 1, $0.01 > p > 0.05$	a 'trend'
Open school boys (n = 100)	11	19	$x^2 = 2.93$, df = 1, $0.10 > p > 0.05$	a 'trend'
TOTAL	24	43	$x^2 = 7.3$, df = 1, $0.01 > p > 0.001$	0.01

Significantly more psychiatric reports than psychological ones appear, probably because Courts and Hearings incline towards the age old authority of medicine, for the links between law and psychiatry are traditional and established.

Thus the boy's file and the running record of the boy's life in the establishment is available and a picture of the facts, offences, past placements, and home, as seen by professionals, begins to emerge. However, the boy may be different to this image in actuality. Prejudging is not helpful save that obvious pitfalls of information are avoided such as politely enquiring for a boy's family when none exists, or a death has recently occurred. The file indeed tells as much about the various report writers and their constructs as about the boy.

The ethical problem of such a file's existence has always been disquieting to the writer as it is to many colleagues. One of the consequences of conviction for the boy is that it lays him open to social work enquiry and the investigation of his family, its secrets and its pain, should such exist. He does not know what is in the file, nor does his family, nor can its data be refuted as its contents are unknown to him. The children's rights movement could demur and the movement for Civil Liberties.

Only the probity of staff protects him, for he is treated in the 'here and now' situation of what the boy actually does and how he behaves in the institution.

Nevertheless, the file is certainly of value to the psychologist in tracing the boy's path through schools, assessment centres, other List D schools or wherever else he has been; and in telling something of the people by whom he has been 'handled' previously. The psychologist's own report will eventually lie with these others and his duty is to help and guard the child, to the best of his power, by it, and to advise on care.

Conscious therefore of the child's right to privacy, yet of the task as psychologist to analyse and advise, he meets the child. This is a two way process. Ginsburg (1972) emphasises the need for professionals to consider the client's view of the interlocutor. 'Who is this person?' 'What right has he to talk to me?' 'Must I answer?' 'Get lost!' The interview is important to the child—in fact his life pattern can be affected—yet to the psychologist it is only one part of his day's work, perhaps forgotten in the process of subsequent interviews with other children and other events. Delicacy to feelings, courtesy, sensitivity to the boy's reactions, listening, as in any social exchange, are essential.

Thus the interview has the orthodoxy of any introduction. The psychologist tells the child his own name, describes his job briefly, although in the institution this is generally well known (as are all other things and people). Then the child tells his name, his address. The initial interview is structured by the *aide-memoire* of the form which is shown as Table 7.3. The details cover a wide range and each could extend into much discussion. The boy is led gently through the various questions without hurry, often stopping to follow his responses and additional information volunteered. Friendly comments accompany the questions while the boy is settling. The questions elicit considerable information and indeed it is on the answers supplied that the data on the present research mainly relies. It may take twenty to thirty minutes to fill the form and during this time the boy is assessing the psychologist and vice versa. A relationship and acquaintenceship is forming. The 'curriculum vitae' apparently does not probe deep, but, as it were, establishes the personal identity and history of the boy.

Subsequently some testing may ensue, changing to a structure of undisturbing and non-personal exchanges to form a stronger bridge of interpersonal knowledge. Usually this may be the Wechsler intelligence scale for children (WISC) or the Wechsler adult intelligence scale (WAIS) for older boys, both having a high intercorrelation with each other. Raven's matrices and the AH4 were also occasionally used. Curiously most boys, unsophisticated in testing techniques and their implications, enjoy this process, apparently completely non-threatened, responding freely and

Table 7.3

Form for initial interview

STRICTLY CONFIDENTIAL

SCOTTISH LIST D SCHOOLS

NORTH EAST PSYCHOLOGICAL SERVICE

Surname	School ....
Christian name	Date of First interview ....
Address	Date of birth ....
....	Age at 1st interview ....
Parents' names and ages F.....M.....	Religion F........M........Pupil........
Place in family	Occupation of parents ....
Referred by	Problem ....
Reason for referral	D of C*...... D of A† ....
Residential Placements with dates	Court (Section............).......
....	Hearing (Section.............).....
....	Date of 1st Hearing ....
....	Social worker (name, address & tel.)
School Welfare Officer	....
....	....

Psychological Tests

*Date of commital by Hearing or Court

†Date of admission to the establishment

often merrily. Even shy, withdrawn and initially hostile boys slowly thaw, interpreting the test as a social game and enjoying it. Encouragement from the psychologist with no pressure promotes the atmosphere of wellbeing. The boy is never allowed to feel he is doing badly as testing stops at his own limits—rather he acquires a sense of achievement.

Intelligence testing is a dirty word to many present day psychologists, the concept of measuring intelligence being deemed invalid, a great deal of time and work being used to no purpose. Vernon (1978), while agreeing that group testing is misused, still argues that individual testing is of value in diagnosing the strengths and weaknesses of backward and highly gifted children. The writer agrees with this view for it is an estimate of the child's potential ability which usually supports the impressionistic assessment of those caring for the child. Moreover if the testing is used as a structured interview where the boy can relate easily to the psychologist it has additional value. The side effects of listening to the boy's words, judging how he assesses problems, how he 'ticks', getting to know him are certainly important in learning about the child. When the British Ability Scales are available these will, it is hoped, have greater flexibility for assessment in that they produce a profile of skills and not merely an intelligence quotient value and performance as in the WISC and WAIS. The new scales will, it is hoped, prove welcome.

For assessment of computational skills, the arithmetic subtest 5 of the Wechsler intelligence scale for children (revised form) is used. This is expressed as a test age score and gives an adequate estimate of the boy's arithmetical ability. For reading age the Vernon graded word reading test is given.

To conclude this screening the boy is asked to write his name and address. Curiously this is singularly revealing, handwriting being sensitive in discriminating various attributes, including academic ability. Some boys can hardly write, and their spelling is guesswork. Others write easily with no problem of spelling. Idiosyncrasies of all varieties appear in this simple process and is possibly the most diagnostic, but not scoreable, of the academic tests used.

To some extent the psychologist is using the boy's own constructs from school to interpret what is happening. The boy understands reading, writing and arithmetic, and 'general knowledge' (which is how he construes the WISC). The carry-over from school experiences defuses his anxiety that the psychologist is 'looking into his head' or that there is a suspicion of enquiry into mental illness. All boys have some good connotations from school, however they may have intermingled with bad. In the introductory interview these 'good' memories are sought out and built on.

The length of the interview, leisurely and friendly, reassuring at all times, allows time for non-verbal mutual assessment. Time may vary from one to two hours. Hurry and brusqueness are avoided. Both sides are picking up cues. From the psychologist's side, body communications (Argyle 1969 and 1975) are silently but consciously interpreted. Hands tell much. Bitten nails, sometimes infected after tearing; torn cuticles; bruising of the nail itself by biting; knuckles, rubbed with scarring subsequently picked at, tell of anxieties. Conversely, well kept and clean nails suggest a calm mind.

Movements of hands during the interview are also informative. Sometimes hand movements tell as much as facial expressions, instantly understood by the interviewer, and adding to what is said, or even replacing verbal communication.

The general appearance of the boy is also informative—his cleanliness or otherwise; for in an institution, although staff also have an interest in the cleanliness of their charges, there is a considerable variation in result. How does he wear his clothes? Food marks on the jersey? Hair rough and hiding his eyes, or combed and shining? Depression is evidenced by identifiable cues and good spirits equally. How does he move? Quickly and with energy or listlessly with drooping bones? Tone of voice? Inaudible or clear, hostile, polite, friendly or reserved.

Distancing is also informative. If the boy sits back in his chair, arms close to his sides, hands hidden, spine rigid, he is probably defensive and self-protecting. If he then begins to lean on the table and let his hands appear and tension releases, his mood is changing. Conversely body movements reflect mental processes and alert the psychologist though nothing is said, a twitching foot, or bitten lip, or cheek or ear pulling, face rubbing, head scratching, shoulder movements.

Eye contact is the most significant interaction and the smile, the frown, the avoidance of glance, or conversely the aggressive stare; the questioning look. The nod of agreement, the mantling of pain and perhaps the tears of a homesick new arrival or of a sad memory from the past.

In short the 'test' materials provide a forum for interpersonal relationships to commence between the child and the psychologist. The pair do not sit silently striving for something to say to each other, the child stonewalling all personal approaches. He is in an interaction he can understand and in which he is willing to participate. Essentially too the boy's privacy is respected. He does not want to talk to a stranger about himself, his family or his past and certainly not at the first interview. He is in compulsory residential care convicted, 'doing time' unwillingly because of offences for which he has been caught, although he knows of other boys with the same actions who are still at home. He does not want his private life to be examined and discussed. 'That's my business.' Perhaps later, when both are known to each other, the boy may come and reveal a problem, and ask for advice about what he might do. But most boys feel their main problem is their incarceration, their removal from home, from friends, from their native streets. The psychologist, part of the imprisonment system, cannot help in their overriding and ever present problem. All he can do, at best, is to try to ameliorate the present situation by his personal presence. The boys know that the psychologist has no administrative power over release, food, clothing, warmth, discipline, staff or themselves. He is perhaps merely a fellow inmate.

The main problem the boys bring is the date of release. 'When do you think . . . ?' 'Will you ask the headmaster . . . ?' This perpetual question revolves endlessly and embraces all their other unrevealed and undiscussed inner thoughts. Few boys feel they have other problems, or at least none they could not solve themselves if they 'got out' and were at liberty to cope with their lives.

The boys who do seek advice come in their own time when they choose. Often their problem is too private to share with anyone but the psychologist who is unattached to the administration and who by now the boy knows well and trusts. 'I want to speak to you.' But this confidence does not grow in a day. The boy weighs up the psychologist's behaviour not only towards himself but to other boys and staff and over extended time.

After the initial interview, or perhaps even later, a written report is prepared for the use of staff and also so that the psychologist has a written record of his assessment for subsequent referrals by himself. Reports are also prepared for a variety of purposes, such as the Court, the Hearings or the boy's social worker, and especially for the psychologist to reconsider when working with the child.

At subsequent interviews other events may occur, and other techniques used as a forum. Many types of personality test are available. Kelly's repertory grid can tell much about the child, but only if the child is willing to engage himself, for some boys find this too threatening, invading as it does the inner sanctum of his feeling for himself and his associates. It cannot be administered in the writer's view unless trust and confidence exist between psychologist and the client and even then reserves are experienced. It is valid only when the child himself wants to learn about himself. Nevertheless, in subsequent study the writer hopes to work on repertory grids with the Wing boys; and always with their consent and approval.

The Rorschach method of personality diagnosis is a process the writer uses frequently and to which boys respond freely. The Rorschach consists of a series of cards where ink blots are shown in random patterns, such as can be seen in clouds and in the glowing embers of a fire. The imagination circles round the shapes and ideas uppermost in the mind appear spontaneously. 'It's two people dancing.' 'It's a lake with sail boats.' 'It's a crocodile sitting in the sun.' Responses are infinitely variable, depending on the constructs in the child's mind. The 'blots' open windows into the fantasies and memories of his inner world. 'It's a knife all rusty with blood.' The object relations technique and the thematic apperception

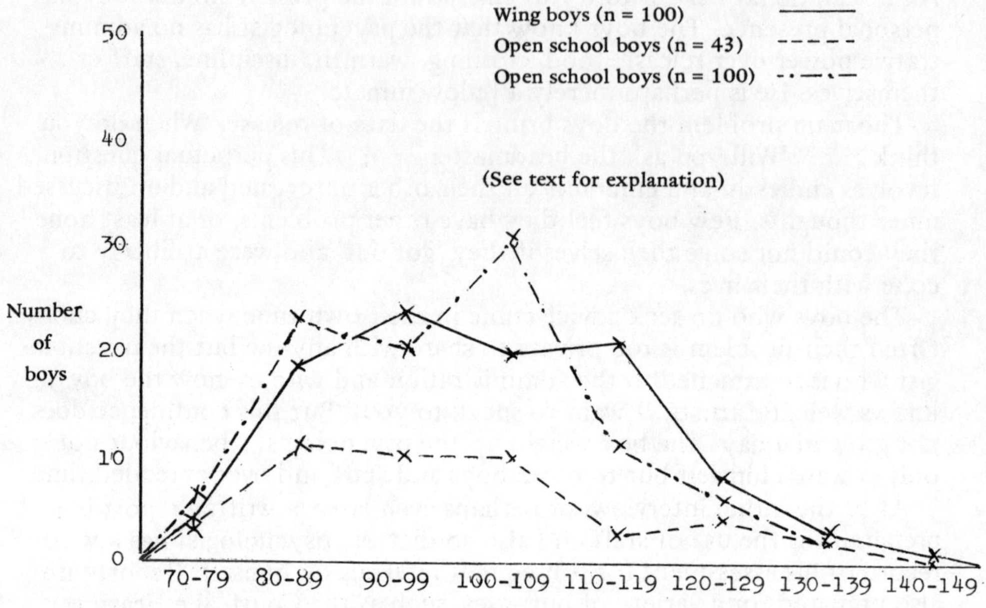

Figure 7.2 WISC and WAIS report scores

Table 7.4

WISC and WAIS report scores

IQ level	70-79	80-89	90-99	100-109	110-119	120-129	130-139	140-149
Wing (n = 100)	4	19	24	20	21	8	3	1
Open school (n = 43)	3	11	10	10	3	4	2	0
Open school (n = 100)	6	23	20	31	11	6	3	0

Number of boys

test are of the same genre.

Space does not permit discussion of other tests. The variety of these is great and the appetite of the boys for what they see as social games is great. Time is what the boys most want from the psychologist—time, the greatest courtesy of all between individuals.

In general, therefore, the boys in both the Open school and in the Wing are friendly and co-operative to an extent not always experienced in normal school by teachers.

Intelligence testing

Comparable numbers of boys have not been achieved for the two groups of boys as the Wechsler intelligence scale for children or the Wechsler adult intelligence scale was not given to all the 100 Open school boys and cannot now be achieved as the boys are now all released.

This was mainly a factor of the toil and time involved and is regretted. The results for the 100 Wing boys are available and these are compared with the results of the testing of the 43 Open school boys for whom testing did occur. Fortunately the numbers in the two groups are large enough to allow legitimate statistical comparison. These may also be compared with the figure for the normal population which is well known.

Intelligence test scores. Figure 7.2 shows that the shapes of the curves of IQ scores are similar. The mean IQ for the Wing boys is 102.60, s.d. 18, and the mean IQ for the Open schools boys is 98.95, s.d. 18.3. Analysis by 't' test show there is no significant difference between the scores ('t' = 1.15, df = 141, $p > 0.10$). The mean score of both groups is, moreover, not statistically different to that in a normal school population, i.e. IQ 100, s.d. 16.

It should be pointed out that there is no reason to believe that any bias operates in the Open school sample. However, as an interesting exercise, the actual IQ testing of the 43 boys was compared with results of all, using an estimated assessmentof the IQ level of the remaining 57 boys well known to the writer. By using a number of indices (reading age, arithmetic age, school reports, social reports and interview data), each boy's intelligence level was estimated and these data combined with those already obtained for the smaller sample to provide the Open school curve. A chi-square test over the seven IQ categories of distribution of test scores for the two groups shows no significant difference between them (x^2 = 7.51, df = 6, $0.30 > p > 0.20$). (Figure 7.2.)

That the cohort of boys is not statistically different to boys in the normal school population is an important finding, denying the previously unchallenged myth that delinquent boys are dull in intelligence. Walter (1978) asserts that the boys in List D Scottish schools which he studied

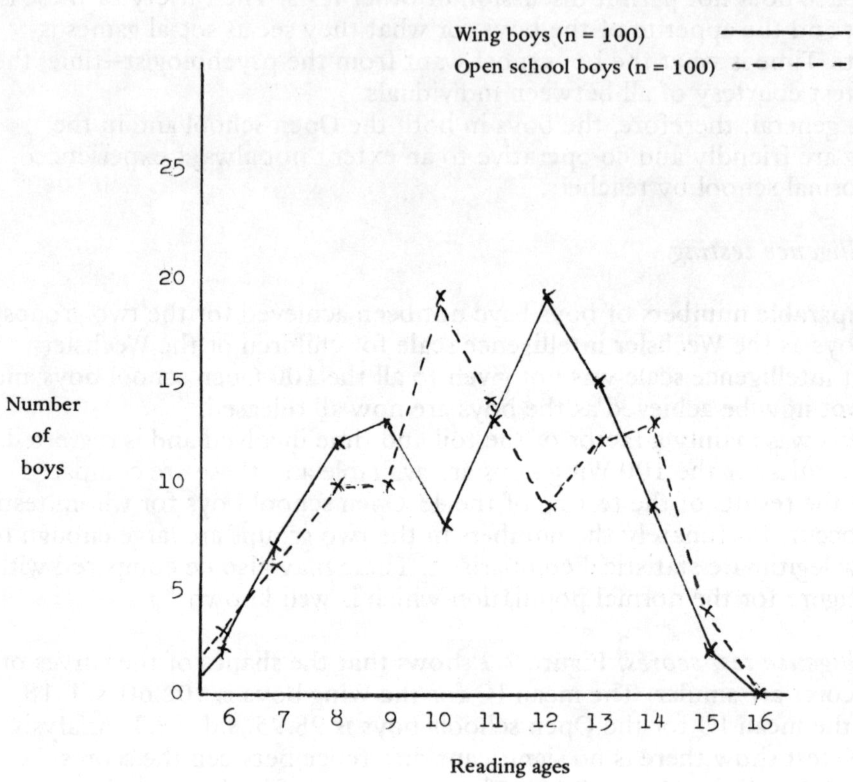

Figure 7.3 Reading ages

Table 7.5
Reading ages

Reading age	6	7	8	9	10	11	12	13	14	15
Wing boys (n = 100)	2	7	12	13	8	13	19	15	9	2
Open school boys (n = 100)	3	6	10	10	19	14	9	12	13	4

't' = 0.12, df = 198, p 0.90 (no significant difference)

were 'mostly in the 80–100 range' though 'at least one boy was in the 60s and one boy was measured at 136'. Walter does not give his sources of information and, if he is a sociologist, is not qualified himself to use IQ tests. Disfavour is done to the boys by such figures, for the population of Dalmore (the school he studied) will not differ substantially from that of Forest for its sources of population are the same. Burt himself (1937) in *The Backward Child* and *The Young Delinquent* (1944) held the same view although allowing, like Walter writing thirty years later, that some did lie outside the 'dull average' range. Field (1971) is also of this view, i.e. that delinquent boys are dull in intelligence.

In fact, examining the figure and table, the present study makes clear that one third of the Wing boys lie above the IQ 110 level with four over 130. All such boys could, with good teaching and motivation, attain Highers, and twelve certainly could be at University Honours student level.

The Open school boys also have scores in this range. From the 43 Open school boys there are 9 boys over IQ 110, i.e. 21 per cent.

The distribution of both groups is skewed somewhat above the mean IQ 100 of the normal population, with a slight advantage in favour of the Wing boys but the difference is not statistically significant ('t' = 1.15, df = 141, $p > 0.10$). (Figure 7.2.)

Reading age. Figure 7.3 shows the reading ages of the boys in both groups. The scores were obtained on the Vernon graded word reading test. The graph indicates that the Wing boys have a higher reading age level than the Open school boys shadowing their apparently slightly higher intelligence level. However, analysis of significance of difference by 't' test does not confirm this. The mean reading age of the Wing boys (n = 100) is 10.76 years and the mean age of the Open school boys (n = 100) is 10.80 years. Obviously there is no significant difference.

In literacy, estimated as being over a reading age of eight years, there are slightly more Wing boys, 21 as compared with 19—a difference not statistically significant. A reading age level of about eight years allows an individual to read simple newspapers, notices in shops, posters and cinema advertisements, etc., but does not go much further. In both groups, therefore, 20 per cent of the boys are poor readers but this in some measure reflects lower intelligence levels in the boys concerned (see Figure 7.2). The boys in the study, however, have a high level of school avoidance (see Table 2.7) and some will be low in academic techniques. Much that they have learnt has been acquired by use and wont and their own initiative in a literate society; and, moreover, most boys attended primary school, school avoidance starting at the secondary level, after obtaining the primary skills.

Opportunities for the poor readers to achieve good literacy while in the

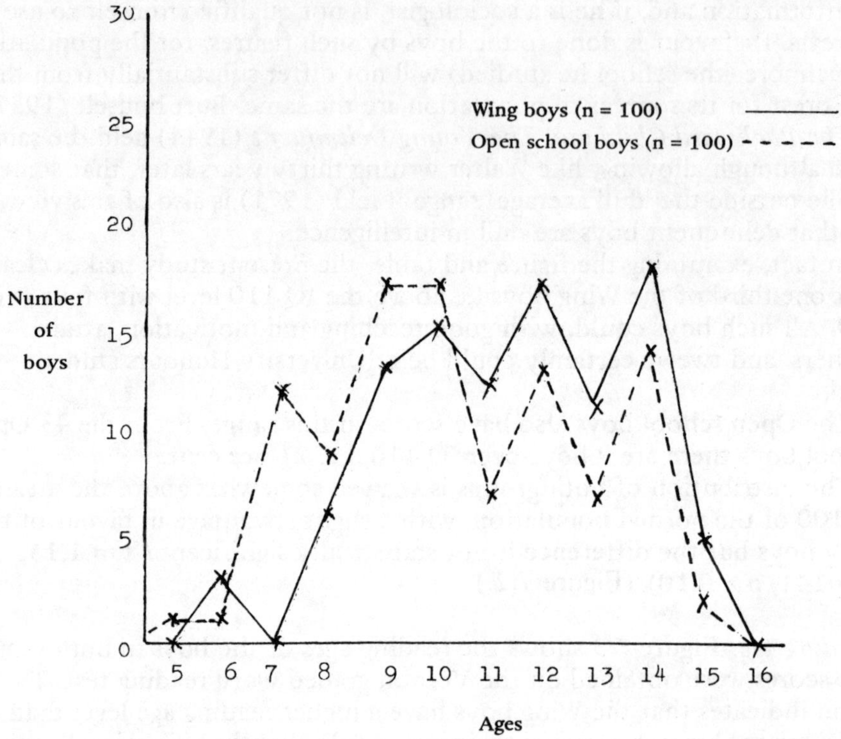

Figure 7.4 Arithmetic ages

Table 7.6

Arithmetic ages

Arithmetic ages	5	6	7	8	9	10	11	12	13	14	15	16
Wing boys (n = 100)	0	3	0	6	13	15	12	17	11	18	5	0
Open school boys (n = 100)	1	1	12	9	17	17	7	13	7	14	2	0

't' = 2.68, df = 198, 0.01 p 0.001 (difference is significant at 0.01 level)

stable situation of compulsory residential care should obviously be given to them for even boys of low intelligence can learn to read, given good, careful and continuous remedial education at a level which they can enjoy and when motivation is aroused. The time 'inside' should allow this fruitful development.

Figure 7.3 demonstrates that the distribution of reading age follows the normal expected curve, with low, average and good readers as would be expected in any school population. A comparative group of 100 boys in the normal school would reveal similar figures, the level of non-readers varying according to the school concerned. There is no evidence of abnormal backwardness in reading age for our two groups of boys.

Literacy is of great importance to boys in compulsory residential establishments in that it is their main link with home, relatives, friends and girlfriends. Weekly letters are written under the guidance of staff. Letters from home are eagerly sought and extreme anxiety accompanies the non-arrival of letters. Boys who receive no letters 'get a read of' letters sent to other boys either as a favour, or bought by sweets or cigarettes, deriving vicarious comfort. Staff note the amount of letters and home solicitude is reckoned by the numbers of letters received. Letters each way, however, are censored by the social work staff and these have incidentally an important role in the staff's knowledge of the boys. The boys, of course, know that letters are censored and sometimes use this method of communicating to the staff their needs, hopes and fears.

Few boys read much in the school. Comics and cowboy novels and the *Sun* and *Mirror* newspapers are the main material. Books, save by a very few boys, are derided. Nevertheless, the teacher or staff member who reads to boys, and tells them stories, is much appreciated. A good book can last for weeks and never tire the listening boys.

Chronological age and reading age. The Wing boys, as shown in Figure 7.1, are divergent in ages and this might be supposed to influence the expectation for their reading ages in comparing them with the Open school boys. The mean chronological age, however, of the Wing boys is 14.236 years and that of the Open school boys is 15.624 years. This difference is not significant so the chronological age can be disregarded.

Arithmetic age. Figure 7.4 shows the arithmetic ages of the boys in both groups. Again the Wing boys appear to have a higher level of attainment than the Open school boys but this is not borne out by statistical analysis. The mean arithmetic age of the Wing boys is 11.39 years and that of the Open school boys is 11.50 years—a difference obviously not significant. Nevertheless, the graph indicates the trend of better numeracy in the Wing boys. Only three Wing boys are below arithmetic age eight compared with 14 Open school boys. Arithmetic age eight is at the level of simple addition and subtraction where simple purchases in shops can be effected and cost of admission to cinema and football grounds calculated. Such boys are capable enough with money as it is important to their needs, and simple addition and subtraction is adequate for them. Multiplication and division is beyond their grasp, esoteric skills they do not use.

However, at arithmetic age eleven plus, where the bulk of the boys lie, numeracy is solid enough for practical needs and 23 Wing boys and 16 Open school boys have arithmetic ages over fourteen years (see Figure 7.4). The distribution of both groups is similar to that which would occur in a normal comprehensive school. Backwardness, as in reading age, is not general through either group.

Arithmetic age and chronological age. As with reading age, the diversity of chronological ages in the Wing and Open school is not significant in difference of means and can be ignored as contaminating the scores.

Handwriting. This is not possible to score objectively, even on a five point scale, as opinion must here influence objectivity. As a projection test it has value, as discussed above, but it is not 'hard' data. In the writer's view it is, however, the most immediate accurate assessment of attainment. It is important to the boys at whatever level of skill, because it is their continuing message–sending alliance with home in their weekly letter writing.

The boys themselves

The foregoing tends to show that both groups of boys are very like each other and also very like the boys in a normal comprehensive school. The cohort is a microcosm, with the normal range of clever, stupid and average children. Intelligence and attainment follow the normal spread as in any population which is selected randomly. The difference is that these boys are 'displaced' and lonely, for they have been exiled from the main stream of children into compulsory residential care, 'open' for the Open school boys and 'closed' for the Wing. They are away from their families, their friends and from girls, missing feminine association—even that of mothers and sisters. They are missing the teenage years of maturation in a normal environment when so much is learned socially through adolescence. These are not rough hooligans, not even 'paper tigers', but lost children like those whom Charles Kingsley describes. Other writers such as Millham et al (1978), Cawson and Martell (1978). West and Farrington (1973) and Dunlop (1974) express the same finding, having worked closely with similar boys in the course of their researches in the schools. In being close to the boys, talking with them and knowing the fragility of their hopes and the depths of their fears, one must deplore their state. Millham calls secure accommodation 'a brief sojourn in an expensive ante-room to the prison system'. The boys wait there with docility and good humour, in the main, and do not resent their keepers, the care staff, the teachers, senior staff and researchers. The sadness of passing formative years in residential establishments cannot, however, be ignored even though the children do not seem resentful. Pat Cawson (1978) writes:

> My research project followed up criminal records of children who were referred but not admitted to the secure units for a year after referral, and a group of admissions were similarly followed up for a year after discharge. Results were precisely those which previous research would have led us to expect: the younger, non-delinquent and less delinquent had a poorer prognosis if admitted than if not admitted. In this context the trends of referral cannot be seen as a healthy state of affairs in the child care service.

But society demands its sacrifices. Parsloe (1978). Children do commit offences. Our children in the List D schools are the ones who are caught. The Wing boys are the ones who did not submit to incarceration, voting with their feet and running away. Millham et al. (1978) declare that 'almost all the candidates for secure places are casualties of the care system'. While this is not true for all the children, it is a view we should consider. The Wing boys' offences initially were the same as those of other children (see Table 2.1) but the ancillary actions resulting from institutionalisation set in motion the train leading to the locked Wing. The primary offences have escalated, because they bucked the system, like the subsequent nails, each at double the price in the horse's shoe, resulting in millions of pounds to be eventually paid, as the cost of compulsory residential placement, both secure and open, is very high.

Conclusion

In the three criteria, IQ score, reading age and arithmetic age, there is no significant difference between the two groups nor are any of the three scores significantly different from those obtaining in a normal comprehensive school.

These findings contradict the myth that delinquent boys are generally dull and backward, and thus different from boys in normal comprehensive schools.

The search for differences between the groups continues to be unavailing, save in the significantly higher number of handicapped fathers in the Wing group; differences in religion; in school refusal (higher for the Open school boys) and in the greater number of previous placements for the Wing boys in compulsory institutions.

8 Follow-up of the boys

The task of following up the boys after release presented difficulties in that no subsequent records are now kept at Social Work Services Group and changes in the administration of the social work departments who have the responsibility to supervise the boys while in residential placement make follow-up difficult. Boys who have fulfilled the full measure of 'sentence' under Section 413 or Section 206(2) are released from supervision completely and no care after release takes place officially. Boys from both sections who are released under licence before their sentence has expired are expected to be supervised by their social worker until this time. Thereafter no official connection remains. Children released by a review Hearing also stay under the care of their social worker until supervision is formally terminated at sixteen years or later in some cases, for supervision can continue until age eighteen. Sometimes, however, supervision is terminated at the review Hearing.

Some regions are more punctilious about aftercare than others, depending on the level of staffing available. The personality of social workers and priority ratings of social work departments also predicates where work choice lies, for in the generic nature of social work many varied and pressing tasks exist, geriatric care, battered wives and babies, children's homes, community development, social security, Court reports—a wide variety of such pressing tasks compete for the social worker's time. Delinquent and maladjusted children may thus come as a low priority. A decade after the inception of the Social Work (Scotland) Act, social workers are less starry-eyed than they were originally and work dissatisfaction is shown by the strikes now arising over conditions of service and pay all over the UK. Adjustment to the professional demands of the service is developing. The time and involvement for boys released from List D schools may seem a heavy commitment and too discouraging in some cases to seem apposite. One social worker related that supervision for released boys comes fifth or sixth in priority and 'often does not make that'.

Nevertheless, the response to the questionnaire sent to the boys' social workers (see Table 8.1) on the later activities of our cohort produced 173 replies for which the writer is grateful. Directors of social work gave permission for area supervisors to be approached and through them the boys' social workers. Naturally many social workers had changed, and some boys have disappeared without trace, but records were obviously searched

Table 8.1

Questionnaire to Social Workers

Scottish List D Schools North East Psychological Service

10 Bayview Road, Aberdeen. Telephone 0224 35978 Date . . . .

Name: . . . .

Date of Birth: . . . .

Date of Release: . . . .

Address at Release: . . . .

Please tick appropriately:

		Yes	*No*	*Unknown*
1	Has the Social Work Department had contact with the boy since release?	. . .	. . .	. . .
2	If below school leaving age, has he attended school satisfactorily?	. . .	. . .	. . .
3	If above school leaving age, is he now gainfully employed?	. . .	. . .	. . .
4	Has he ever been employed since release?	. . .	. . .	. . .
5	Has he been involved in a Job Creation Scheme?	. . .	. . .	. . .
6	Has he married?	. . .	. . .	. . .
7	Has he children?	. . .	. . .	. . .
8	Has he had offences since release?	. . .	. . .	. . .

		under 2 months	*under 6 months*	*under 1 year*	*unknown*
9	If so, how long after release?	. . .	. . .	. . .	. . .

OFFENCES

10	With what type of offence?	*1st*	*2nd*	*3rd*	*4th*	*multiple*
1)	R.T.A.	. . .	. . .	. . .	. . .	. . .
2)	Theft					
3)	Violence	. . .	. . .	. . .	. . .	. . .
4)	Breach of the Peace	. . .	. . .	. . .	. . .	. . .
5)	Other (please specify)					

11	Result of prosecution:	*1st*	*2nd*	*3rd*	*4th*	*multiple*
1)	Return to Forest	. . .	. . .	. . .	. . .	. . .
2)	Not Guilty	. . .	. . .	. . .	. . .	. . .
3)	Fine	. . .	. . .	. . .	. . .	. . .
4)	Young Offenders	. . .	. . .	. . .	. . .	. . .
5)	Borstal	. . .	. . .	. . .	. . .	. . .
6)	Prison	. . .	. . .	. . .	. . .	. . .
7)	Probation	. . .	. . .	. . .	. . .	. . .
8)	Conditional discharge .	. . .	. . .	. . .	. . .	. . .
9)	Unconditional discharge	. . .	. . .	. . .	. . .	. . .
10)	Community Service . .	. . .	. . .	. . .	. . .	. . .
11)	Other disposal					

12 Other information, e.g. hospitalisation . . . .

Date of reply . . . . Social Worker's Name, Address: . . . .

Telephone . . . .

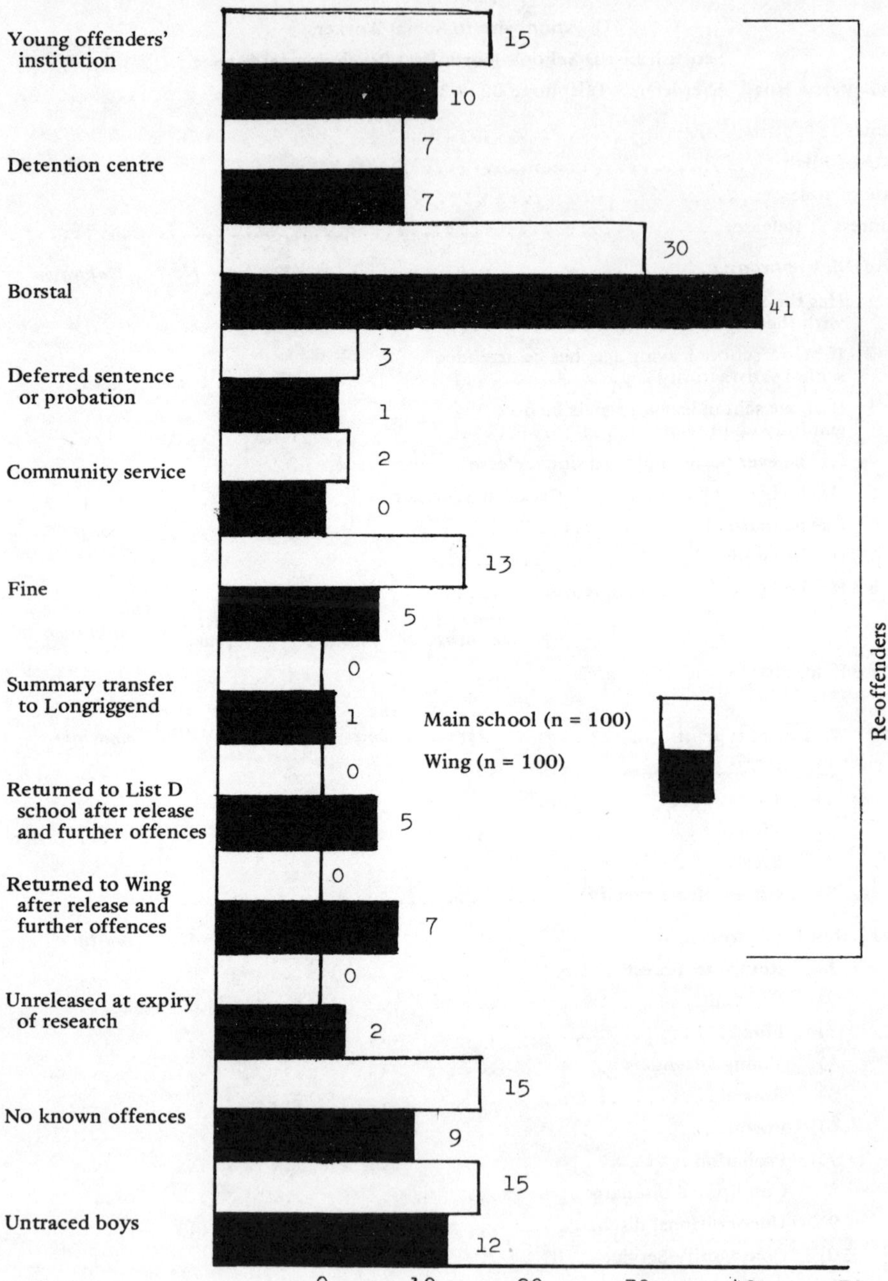

Figure 8.1 Follow-up of boys after release

and a greater response than expected eventuated. Forest School records were also searched.

Table 8.2 shows the data discovered. It also shows what happened to the boys and the number (in the different categories) of disposals from the Courts and Hearings (see also Figure 8.1).

Table 8.2

Follow-up of boys, sentenced and non-offending, at the date when the research closed

Category	Wing (n = 100)	Open school (n = 100)	Chi-square test	Level of significance
Young offenders	10	15	$x^2 = 0.75$, df = 1, $p > 0.10$	n.s.
Detention centre	7	7	–	n.s.
Borstal	41	30	$x^2 = 1.43$, df = 1, $p > 0.10$	n.s.
Suspended sentence or probation	1	3	–	n.s.
Community service	0	2	–	n.s.
Fine	5	13	$x^2 = 2.99$, df = 1, $0.10 > p > 0.05$	'trend'
Transferred to Longriggend summarily	1	0	–	–
Returned to List D school after release and further offences	5	0	–	–
Returned to Wing after release and further offences	7	0	–	–
(Reoffenders)	(77)	(70)	$x^2 = 0.92$, df = 1, $p > 0.10$	n.s.
Unreleased at expiry of research	2	0	–	–
No known offences	9	15	$x^2 = 0.85$, df = 1, $p > 0.10$	n.s.
Untraced	12	15	–	–
TOTAL	100	100		

Thus 70 Wing boys and 52 Open school boys are back in custody after release. The trend for more Open school boys to receive fines rather than custody disposal (13 as contrasted with 5) is possibly a factor of 'labelling' militating against the Wing boys but the difference does not reach significance.

The reconviction rate of 77 per cent in the Wing is not significantly different from that discovered by Dunlop (1974), Millham et al (1975–1978) and Cawson (1978) for secure units in England. The 70 per cent reconviction rate of the Open school boys is somewhat higher than that observed in the Dunlop (1974) study of English open schools (Community Homes with Education on the premises), but not significantly so. Both levels of reoffending in the Wing and Open school present a gloomy picture and deepen the impression that both sets of boys have passed through a 'criminogenic experience' in Pat Cawson's words (1978) and certainly not a reformative one, despite the good efforts of the staff working with both groups. Moreover, the level of reconviction for both groups of boys is not significantly different, 77 per cent in the Wing and 70 per cent in the Open school ($x^2 = 0.01$, df = 1, $p > 0.10$). Figures after Borstal are similar, 75 per cent after one year and 93 per cent after four years (Bannister 1975).

The number of boys with no known offence (9 in the Wing and 15 in the Open school) is not significantly different between the groups or from that found in the English studies. It does, however, clearly demonstrate how ineffective in the prevention of recidivism the placements in compulsory residential care have been on the total cohort of 200 boys. A level of remission at this level could have resulted spontaneously in any case.

It is of interest (see Table 8.2) that about the same number of boys in each group have reoffended and gone to young offenders' institutions. Punishment, not treatment, is emphasised there and the sentence can be as short as three months. It is the 'short, sharp shock' treatment in these instances and is somewhat dreaded by the boys but preferred to Borstal as it is over quickly.

Borstal is not dissimilar in nature to the experiences the boys have already had. 'Doing your Borstal' is a badge of maturity to some boys. Brothers, cousins and older friends have gone and survived and, as has been said above, when Wing boys get to Borstal they will know, or know of, most of the inmates there. The Open school boys, less sophisticated, may find it harder but in the aftermath it is a finishing school which takes the boy to manhood. Over age twenty-one, offences fall away as the boy marries, has children and responsibilities, and settles down (Trasler 1970, Reiss 1979). It is not, very probably, the sentence which reforms the boys but wives and families of their own—full time loving and exigent 'social workers'.

Suspended sentences and fines are regarded favourably by the boys but unhappily many of the boys go on, as the months pass, to further offences and then to young offenders or Borstal. Community service (two boys from the Open school) is a new form of training at the present time (1979), the outcome of which is not yet observable.

No boys from the Open school were in Longriggend at the time of the expiry of this study, as far as is known by the writer, since over a year in all cases and sometimes up to three years had elapsed since the boys left Forest. Offenders will have passed through Longriggend or prison on remand and will now have passed through further custody or still be undergoing it. The one Wing boy in Longriggend (see Figure 8.1) had been transferred from the Wing on account of unruly behaviour.

The 100 boys of the Open school group took two years to accumulate for the study but the 100 Wing boys took three years, the population there being much smaller. Thus the last boy released from the Open school has been away one full year, but two of the Wing boys are still there and some have only recently been released. Sadly, as will be shown later, many Wing boys are back in the penal system within weeks.

Boys below school leaving age

Few or no boys left Forest Open school below school leaving age as it is a 'senior school' and boys wish to remain there until they are able to obtain work and avoid return to normal school. The Wing boys, however, are in some cases released before the school leaving age, since they may have entered at thirteen or fourteen years of age. Those are the ones shown in Table 8.1 who were returned to the Wing or to other List D schools after release and further offences. Indeed no boys from the cohort in this study below school leaving age made a successful re-entry into normal school.

These unhappy children left the Wing with good intentions of returning to school, but after a few days or hours of attendance there they did not return, discouraged and isolated, hung about the streets, becoming involved in further offences and eventually were placed in assessment centres or Longriggend. They are 'different' to ordinary school boys and are not accepted. They have lost their place both socially and in school work.

The Wing makes valiant attempts to reintegrate the boys by means of their social workers visiting their schools and involving the aid of headmasters, guidance staff and teachers. This has been in vain so far.

A new demarche is now being pursued in Forest by the writer whereby the local Child Guidance Centre is to be invoked through the medium of the principal psychologist who could oversee the case personally and provide the boy with cover, either in a special unit or in a clinic. The boy would thus not be exposed to the rough and tumble of the normal school in a low stream class, but be given individual care by the Educational Psychological Service. All principal psychologists are now being approached by the List D psychological service to evoke this aid. It would be a specialist care for the returning children, each according to his need. It would mean an extra burden for the Educational Psychological Services, but with their particular skills and knowledge of local provision they are well suited to provide help, shelter and family therapy to the boys. The pilot scheme is now in operation and high hopes are entertained of it.

The following contrasting case histories illustrate the situation of children returning from List D school to normal school.

Psychological report

Jimmie left the Wing aged fifteen. He was a clever boy, IQ 130, nice looking with clear skin, dark curly hair and striking blue eyes graced with long dark eyelashes. He spoke pleasantly and had an agreeable presence. His mother was dead and his family had remarried to a woman with four children of her own who detested Jimmie.

On return home he tried to reintegrate himself with his family but fruitlessly. Within a week he had been put out of the house by the stepmother and was 'living rough' helped by hand-outs from the father. Obviously he did not attend school, and drifted with other truants round the town. He quickly became involved with a 'punk' group playing at local discos and made himself useful to them, running errands and helping with their show. Soon he had acquired the 'gear', safety pins through his ears and festooning his clothes, together with lavatory chains ad lib on his person. He learned too the trick of vomiting at will and could also make his nose bleed. In short he built himself into the punk cult enthusiastically, giving the group his total commitment.

Jimmie's social worker was perturbed but helpless. Minor offences and school refusal eventually allowed her to corral him and take him to a Hearing. In the assessment centre his vomiting was a sensation to staff and also frightening and he was quickly transferred to another List D school in the west of Scotland, happily not in a secure unit. There he was out of the punk scene and quickly lost the insigniae. His bright intelligence and ability to adapt stood him in good stead and there his wish to join the Navy was fostered by the headmaster and staff. He is now in a Naval Training School in England according to his own ambition. His family difficulties will not now encroach on him, nor will the need of school, being over sixteen. Now the boy has a chance.

The difficulties of return from the Wing to home were insuperable for this boy on his own. The new hope from the Child Guidance Service care might have saved him initially had it been available.

By contrast, another boy released at age fifteen to return to school could not do so, being acutely school phobic. Like Jimmie he was also 'living rough' in that his parents put him out of the house because of school refusal. He too had minor offences and landed in the assessment centre afflicted with an allergy which took the form of inflamed and oozing sores all over his body. He was taken back to the Wing and there recovered. At a case conference a principal educational psychologist of the region attended and offered to take the boy into his local centre on a part time basis on release. The boy accepted gratefully, attended the centre regularly and happily and his reintegration into the community and employment proceeded peacefully.

The co-operation of List D psychological services with the regional psychological services can thus link together care for the children and hopefully prevent wastage into the penal system.

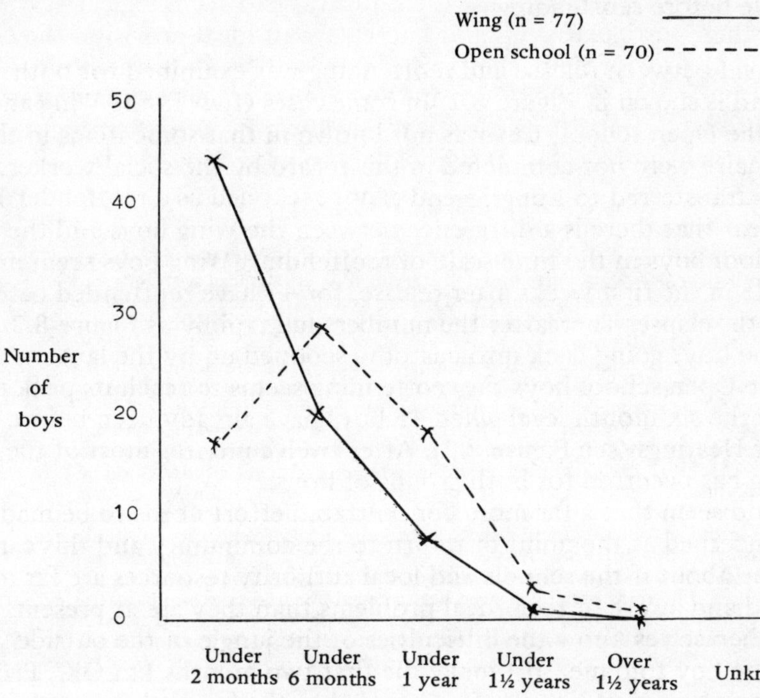

Figure 8.2 Time scale of reoffending

Table 8.3

Time scale of reoffending

	Under 2 months	Under 6 months	Under 1 year	Under 1½ years	Over 1½ years	Unknown
Wing (n = 77)	44	20	8	1	0	4
Open school (n = 70)	17	28	18	3	1	3

Time scale before reoffending

The interval between release and reoffending was examined for both groups and is shown in Figure 8.2. In some cases (four in the Wing and three in the Open school) this was not known in that some items in the questionnaire were not completed in this regard by the social workers. (The boy transferred to Longriggend is not reckoned as a reoffender.)

It is clear that there is a difference between the Wing boys and the Open school boys in the time scale of reoffending. Wing boys seem most vulnerable in the first weeks after release, for 44 have reoffended before two months elapse. Thereafter the numbers fall rapidly as Figure 8.2 shows, the boys going back into custody, scooped up by the law.

For the Open school boys the reoffending seems to reach its peak more slowly to the six month level when 45 boys have already been before the Courts or Hearings (see Figure 8.2). After twelve months most of the reoffending has occurred for both groups of boys.

It would seem that a far more concentrated effort needs to be made by all concerned at the point of return to the community and this can only come about if the schools and local authority resources are far more integrated and aware of reciprocal problems than they are at present.

Boys themselves know the difficulties of the jungle of the outside world. One boy told me, 'If I make the first two months I'm OK'. Problems are reintegration into the family, used to the boy's absence; the finding of a job, already labelled by List D conviction; the difficulty of finding a decent girlfriend in that her family is liable to forbid association due to the List D record; the taunting of the peer group who challenge the returning boy to prove he is a 'hard man'; the temptation to join other boys 'going robbing' and the challenge of being teased as 'being chicken' if he refuses. And continually the presence of the Police at the door who ask for an alibi when any crime in the neighbourhood occurs, as the boys are classed as 'known criminals' in the Police records. The opportunity to obtain alcohol is also inviting and friends offer drinks in welcome. Often the first party is the last because, unused to drink, unruly behaviour is probable.

Sheltered by the institution and dependent on its discipline, the boy's own initiative has grown weak. His good resolutions melt away on release and he floats, almost helplessly, into the prison system. However, if the boy can stabilise in freedom, with a job, a steady girlfriend and a place to live, he has a chance. But he needs help.

The mentally handicapped

There are a few mentally handicapped boys in both groups. Figure 7.2

shows the boys' IQ and indicates this clearly. Tom, of the Open school group, is such a boy. The psychological report is reproduced here, written eight months after he entered Forest. The boy entered Borstal within one month of leaving Forest and will probably become a recidivist prison inmate. This difficult, pathetic and uncontrolled boy would surely be better placed in a mental hospital or sheltered workshop.

Psychological testing

1966	MH2 (assessment of mental handicap)	IQ 78 (Terman Merrill Form L-M)	
1967	MH2 (assessment of mental handicap)	IQ 74 (Child Guidance Centre)	
1972	Wechsler intelligence scale for children	IQ 71 (Child Guidance Centre)	
	Reading age (Burt)	under 7 years	
1975	Reading age (Burt)	7.6 years	Assessment centre
	Arithmetic	poor	
	Spelling age	6.6 years	
1976	Vernon graded word reading test		
	Reading age	8 years	Forest School
	Arithmetic test age (Wechsler sub-tests)	7 years	
	Handwriting	poor	

Report

Tom was a difficult child from an early age. His primary school at age 6 referred him to the educational psychological service for investigation as to mental handicap and he was assessed at IQ 78 in 1966 and a year later as IQ 74. He was then placed in special school but was there found too difficult to contain and was transferred to a school for maladjusted children. After two years of difficulties there he was found intolerable and placed in a further school of the same nature. At age twelve he was returned to his parents and again tried in his former special school. This also failed and he was eventually placed in a junior List D school, proceeding, after this had also broken down, to an assessment centre, finally arriving in Forest.

Reports on the boys in all these placements have been unfavourable, 'vicious, provocative, in a continual state of tension . . . requires psychiatric investigation; unpredictable, difficult'.

Tom has four brothers all of whom have been 'in trouble'. One had run the gamut of junior and senior List D schools, detention centre, Borstal and young offenders' institution. The father is unemployed and there is a suggestion in the social enquiry report that he is criminal in a minor way. The mother is non-wage earning. Both parents, according to Tom's social worker's report, found Tom 'out of parental control' and 'wanted him away'.

The boy thus comes from a disadvantaged family, is mentally handicapped and has been continually rejected by succeeding institutions. His social worker in the report which brought Tom to Forest writes, 'Tom is an open faced boy, with an almost convincing friendly style, supported by a falsified smile'. Indeed this 'smile' is a characteristic of institutionalised children who vainly attempt to make relationships with the professional caring staff who have little time to respond, busy with duties, and continually changing as duty shifts change–'too ready, undifferentiating friendliness'. This 'smile' was also observed in my interview with Tom, but here it was used as a screen which was almost impenetrable, meaningless and disturbing, conveying no personal interaction. The mechanical nature of the 'smile' seemed to evidence inner emptiness, or perhaps despair.

Tom is a child, who is himself damaged and has a damaging effect on the institutions where he has been placed. When he was finally excluded at age twelve from the special school his offences had been 'openly masturbating in front of a woman teacher in class' and 'drinking in the sheds of the school playground'.

In my professional view this boy should not be in a List D school. He has no criminal charges against him, merely displeasing social behaviour. Mental handicap underlying poor social understanding however has made such a child unacceptable in any institution where other children are also being educated so he is always being moved on. Real offences such as theft or violence might conceivably be more tolerable. Placement of a boy like Tom is obviously very difficult but a List D school is not an appropriate solution when other disposals have failed. It should not be used 'as a dustbin' either for Tom's sake, or its own.

Tom is now nearly sixteen and has passed eight months in Forest. He has been less of a problem than might have been supposed. The structure of the school has been supportive to him and he has conformed. His future, after release, must cause concern.

Tom is a difficult case and the prognosis for him in the community must be poor. The psychological tests, listed above, indicate his mental handicap. His literacy is minimal. His social skills are poor. It is probable that Tom should proceed after Forest to a sheltered workshop where he can learn such skills as would enable him to achieve employment.

Consultation with Tom's social worker is sought and a case discussion of all concerned with Tom's welfare should be convened shortly.

Postscript

Tom was in Borstal within weeks of release from Forest.

A further case, from the Wing, is Jimmy with an IQ of 64 (WISC). He received special care in the Wing, sheltered and protected from other boys because he was 'different'. On release, after several leaves, he quarrelled with his mother and was put out of the house. He resumed his habit of glue sniffing 'to the danger of his life'. His brother and an older lad killed an elderly neighbour and then burned the house when under the influence of glue. Jimmy declared himself to be a party to the crime falsely, 'wasting the time of the police', before he was exculpated by alibi.

His supervision order was terminated and the boy placed in a young offenders' institution in that he was 'failing to respond to supervision from his social worker', despite more than ordinary care and attention.

Mentally handicapped boys like these invoke prison treatment when hospital or sheltered workshops might be their lot. But there their incongruous behaviour makes them unacceptable. Only the prisons cannot refuse them when all others fail. But how hard therefore is the task of the penal system!

The influence of the family situation

It could be supposed that the intact family could help the boys to cope with the problems of freedom. Impressionistically this would appear to be so. Yet when the boys' families are counted, doubts appear. For the Wing boys the intact nuclear family appears to correlate with non-reoffending for, of the nine boys with no further offences, eight have intact families and only one has a non-intact family. It would be fascinating to visit these non-reoffending boys personally and assess the reasons for their success. One boy from the Wing had a stable pleasant personality, was highly intelligent, had a self-employed father and mother, non-delinquent siblings, went straight into employment with his father, and had a girlfriend in an 'A' level class at school. Do all 'successful' boys need these criteria?

By contrast, the picture is less cut and dried in the Open school group. Of the fifteen boys who did not reoffend, nine had intact families and six had non-intact families, a difference not statistically significant (see Table 8.3).

Table 8.4

Non-reoffending boys and their families, intact and non-intact

Non-reoffenders	Intact family	Non-intact family	Chi-square test	Level of significance
Wing (n = 9)	8	1	–	n.s.
Open school (n = 15)	9	6	–	n.s.
TOTAL (n = 24)	17	7	$x^2 = 3.84$, df = 1 $p < 0.05$	0.05

It does, nevertheless, appear to hold that for the total number of non-reoffenders there is a significant difference between intact and non-intact families but not for the individual groups. It can therefore be assumed that a boy is helped by his nuclear family to avoid further 'trouble'. But such successfully cherished boys are few in the total cohort as the following information will show.

Reoffending boys

A more definite lack of significant differentiation between intact and non-intact families obtains with boys who reoffend, as indicated in Tables 8.5 and 8.6. Chapter 3 gave evidence that intact and non-intact families are almost evenly divided (50 in the Open school and 55 in the Wing are intact) so there is no significant weighting either way in this respect.

Table 8.5

Wing reoffenders and their families

Disposal by Court or Hearing	Number of boys (n = 77)	Intact family	Non-intact family
Young offenders' institution	10	7	3
Detention centre	7	4	3
Borstal	41	22	19
Suspended sentence	1	1	0
Fine	5	3	2
Transferred to Longriggend from the Wing summarily	1	1	0
Return to List D school	5	2	3
Return to Forest	7	4	3
TOTAL	77	44	33

Table 8.6

Open school reoffenders and their families

Disposal by Court or Hearing	Number of boys (n = 70)	Intact family	Non-intact family
Young offenders' institution	15	7	8
Detention centre	7	3	4
Borstal	30	14	16
Suspended sentence	3	1	2
Community service	2	2	0
Fine	13	6	7
TOTAL	70	33	37

When the number of reoffending boys of intact and non-intact families are compared the difference in numbers is not significant as shown below.

Table 8.7

Reoffenders, intact and non-intact families compared

Reoffending boys	Intact families	Non-intact families	Chi-square test	Level of significance
Wing (n = 100)	44	33	$x^2 = 2.1$, df = 1, $p > 0.10$	n.s.
Open school (n = 100)	33	37	–	n.s.
TOTAL	77	70	$x^2 = 0.92$, df = 1, $p > 0.10$	n.s.

The result is surprising in that it could be supposed that an intact family would have a favourable influence on a boy's behaviour and in the judgements of Courts and Hearings. However, the group of boys is highly selected by reason of previous convictions and these continue as before after release, for the majority, irrespective of family situation.

The nature of reoffending

In Chapter 2 the types of offences by the boys were analysed. Table 2.1 demonstrated that the charges against the boys were not significantly different between the groups and also tended to show that offences were mostly petty theft and car theft. In truancy alone the difference was significant.

Analysis of the reoffending after release showed a changed and less benign picture (see Table 8.8). Information derives from the data supplied by the boys' social workers in the questionnaire discussed above.

Table 8.8

Comparative analysis of reoffending charges after release

Type of offence	Wing boys (n = 77)	Open school boys (n = 70)	Chi-square test	Level of significance
Police assault (stabbing) (4 year sentence)	1	0	–	n.s.
Rape (4 year sentence)	1	0	–	n.s.
Car theft without other offences	5	7	–	n.s.
Theft, housebreaking, opening lockfast premises*	33	32	–	n.s.
Car theft, Road Traffic Act offences, Theft*	22	22	–	n.s.
Assault*	7	24	$x^2 = 9.78$, df = 1 $p < 0.001$	0.001
Breach of the peace *	6	25	$x^2 = 12.36$, df = 1, $p < 0.001$	0.001
Malicious damage *	0	2	–	n.s.
Fire raising	1	0	–	n.s.
Extortion by threat	0	1	–	n.s.
Theft and reset	0	1	–	n.s.
Failing to meet supervision order and recall to young offenders	1	0	–	n.s.
Unknown	6	5	–	n.s.
Total number of reoffending boys	77	70	$x^2 = 0.92$, df = 1, $p > 0.10$	n.s.

*Although the categories are discrete some boys have charges in more than one category.

Offences before and after Forest compared

Violence. When the offences after release are compared with those before entry into Forest, interesting differences emerge. Two Wing boys have serious charges. One stabbed a policeman repeatedly when resisting arrest and is now serving a four year sentence. A second boy is doing a four year sentence for rape. No such serious charges appear for the Open school boys; nor were there any comparable offences in either group before entry into Forest. Little emphasis should perhaps be placed on these two cases as they are not statistically significant in numbers and could be accounted for by chance.

Notable in Table 8.8 is the significantly higher level of charges for assault in the ex-Open school boys, the ex-Wing boys showing a milder level. Similarly, breach of the peace charges are significantly higher in the ex-Open school boys than in the ex-Wing boys. The suggestion therefore emerges that the ex-Wing boys are less aggressive than the ex-Open school boys after release.

Analysis of cases of assault in both groups before and after the Forest experience was undertaken (see Tables 2.1 and 8.9) but analysis by the chi-square test of comparative significance showed there were no real differences, although the difference for the ex-Open school boys nearly achieved significance. The suggestion emerges that the ex-Open school boys became more aggressive after Forest than on entry.

Table 8.9

Comparison of frequency of assault charges before and after Forest

	Number of assaults before Forest	Number of assaults after Forest	Chi-square test	Level of significance
Wing boys	10	7	$x^2 = 0.25$, df = 1, $p > 0.10$	n.s.
Open school boys	15	24	$x^2 = 2.04$, df = 1, $p > 0.10$	approaching significance

Car theft without other offences. In both groups this is not significantly different in frequency before and after Forest (see Table 8.8).

Theft. This offence has diminished greatly in both groups. Before entry to Forest about 90 per cent of boys in both groups carried this charge but only about 30 per cent of the reoffending boys. Probably, being older after release and mostly employable with insurance papers, their temptation towards pilfering decreases. If unemployed the boys are now eligible for social security benefits.

Car theft combined with other offences. This appears approximately constant for the ex-Open school boys on reoffending, but has diminished significantly in the ex-Wing group, although the older boys are not yet eligible for a driving licence or wealthy enough to own a car. It is, however, curious that the ex-Wing boys have fewer such offences than the ex-Open school boys in that an inverse situation obtained before entry to the Wing (see Table 8.10).

Table 8.10

Car theft and other offences before and after Forest

Car theft, Road Traffic Act offences and theft	Before	After	Chi-square test	Level of significance
Wing	37	22	$x^2 = 4.714$, df = 1, $p > 0.05$	0.05
Open school	25	22	–	n.s.

Fire raising. This seems to have almost disappeared among the reoffending boys.

New offences. Some of the charges listed before entry to Forest do not reappear, such as glue sniffing and truancy. Alcohol, probably accounting for most of the charges of breach of the peace and assault, has presumably replaced the juvenile glue. Truancy disappears at the magic age of sixteen. New charges, however, appear such as *extortion by threat* (one Open school boy) and *theft and reset* (also from the Open school).

Failure to fulfil the requirements of the supervision order. Jimmy, the mentally handicapped boy discussed earlier in this chapter, was such a case.

Unknown offences. Some social workers failed to state the offence committed in the questionnaire but supplied the disposal of the Court. So the nature of the crime is not revealed.

Summary of offences

The Wing boys have a lower level of assault and breach of peace charges on reoffending than the Open school boys, but among their number are two serious charges, police assault and rape. The Wing boys now steal fewer cars than the Open school boys. Both groups have a lower level of theft. New charges, reset and extortion, appear in the Open school group.

The impression that the Wing boys have become less antisocial than the other group is clearly given. In the main they appear less angry and quieter, the small numbers and individual care of the Wing probably having been of benefit to them. Recidivism, as has been shown, is not significantly different.

Employment of boys after release

Obviously employment will be helpful for boys after release from Forest in providing them with a livelihood and preventing them from committing further offences. Moreover, if the boy is employed and does offend, it might be supposed to influence decisions by the law on his disposal in his favour.

Tables 8.11 and 8.12 analyse the employment situation and its relation to the disposal of the boys if they reoffend.

Table 8.11

Employment and events after release: Open school boys

Open school boys (n = 100)		Employed at any time since release	Never employed	Unknown
Young offenders' institution or detention centre	(22)	16	4	2
Borstal	(30)	19	6	5
Deferred sentence, probation or community service	(5)	5	0	0
Fine	(13)	9	3	1
Unknown	(15)	0	0	15
No offences	(15)	13	0	2
TOTAL	(100)	62	13	25

Table 8.12

Employment and events after release: Wing boys

Wing boys (n = 100)		Employed at any time since release	Never employed	Unknown
Young offenders' institution or detention centre	(17)	3	12	2
Borstal	(41)	10	18	13
Deferred sentence	(1)	1	0	0
Fine	(5)	3	2	0
Longriggend	(1)	0	0	1
Below school leaving age	(12)	0	0	12
Unknown	(12)	0	0	12
No offences	(9)	6	0	3
Unreleased so far	(2)	0	0	2
TOTAL	(100)	23	32	45

The Open school boys have a significantly higher level of employment than the Wing boys. Similarly, the boys known to have never been employed are significantly more numerous in the Wing group. Nevertheless, employment does not appear to keep the Open school boys out of

Borstal or young offenders' institutions (see Table 8.11) 32 Wing boys as opposed to 13 Open school boys have never been employed before further incarceration (see Table 8.11 and 8.12). However, employed Open school boys sometimes do receive fines, although the difference between employed and unemployed boys who are fined is not significant. Perhaps indeed the nine employed boys who were fined (see Table 8.11) might have had penal sentences if they had been unemployed.

In this regard it must be remembered that many Wing boys have re-offended (see Figure 8.2) within two months of release and have had little chance to be employed. The time scale of reoffending is obviously very relevant in the discussion of employment.

Study of Tables 8.11 and 8.12 shows that the Open school boys have a higher level of employment than the Wing boys, relating to the swifter re-entry of the Wing boys to the penal system, or back to the List D world (see Figure 8.2). Probably the problem of 'labelling' also prejudices against the Wing boys being given employment. They are caught in a catch 22 situation—a vicious circle.

Untraced boys

Reference back to Table 8.2 shows that 12 boys in the Wing and 15 in the Open school cannot be traced. Two boys in the study are not yet released. The prognosis for these latter cannot be known, so the figures for 'unknown' futures are more truly 14 for the Wing and 15 for the Open school—a difference not significant.

The loss of knowledge for the untraced boys is unfortunate but inevitable. Some boys disappear, leaving their native town and losing contact with their social worker. Some social workers leave their posts. Files are sometimes lost or misplaced. Boys released from supervision also have no further contact with the social worker and may or may not have done well or been in further 'trouble'. It is, however, likely that in the latter event their record will follow them, but not necessarily to the knowledge of their former social worker. Moreover, some few social workers may not have been able to return a vexatious, possible irritating questionnaire, overburdened with other tasks. The aid from Polmont on the boys from the psychologist there was invaluable.

Letters back to the school bring news of the boys, the yellow prison paper carrying its own pathos. An example is illustrated on the following page. Telephone calls also occur, the boy seeking reassurance in a lonely world from a security he has experienced as caring towards him. News also travels concerning ex-pupils by way of new boys arriving from sorting houses of Longriggend and the assessment centres. Relatives, brothers or cousins, themselves delinquent, also carry news. The young recidivist 'criminals', as has been said before, are an elitist bunch, few in number and somewhat closely integrated, drifting by misfortune through the junior system to the senior and on to the penal. Happily, in their early twenties, they vanish into the normal population save for a very small minority (Trasler 1970).

Meehan's (1978) book, Boyle (1978) and McVicar (1974) are autobiographies of such professional criminals, the two former having both had national publicity.

NORTH WING

H.M. INSTITUTION,
BRIGHTONS,
Nr. FALKIRK,
FK2 OAB.

Dear Mrs F

Petrie Roddy here with a
few lines to ask how you are keeping
I am sorry that I have not written
before but I am just setling in here.
I got your postcard when I was in
Longgrigend. Well how are things at
? alright I hope I wish I was
still there, but it was my own fault
This place is not to bad though.
I am working in the textiles making
denims on a sewing machine (just
like the ragtrade) Please tell Stan, Mr
Mac and all the boys and Staff
I was asking for them. Well I will
close for now please write back

Love
Roddy

The twelve untraced Wing boys

Close analysis of the reasons for not being able to trace these twelve boys revealed various causes.

Three boys, released within the six months prior to the expiry of the study, had no return made by their social workers. These were from Strathclyde where social workers are notoriously overburdened and staff is not at full strength.

Four boys, from other areas, also had no returns made. They had been released from one and a half to two years.

The social worker of an Edinburgh boy reported that the boy had lost contact with him since supervision had been terminated.

Two boys had left their homes and no address was known to their social worker.

One boy was not traced in his local social work department, his social worker having left and no trace of his file was found by the area supervisor.

Of one boy the social work department responded, 'John has not been seen since release nor was it possible to allocate him to any social worker'.

Summary

Follow-up of the boys after release was achieved by means of a questionnaire sent to the social workers of the released boys. Further information came from the principal psychologist at Polmont where boys go for Borstal assessment. Information was obtained on 173 boys.

77 boys of the Wing group (n = 100) had reoffended, of whom 70 were again in compulsory residential placement, 59 in the penal system and 12 in the juvenile system. Five had fines and one a suspended sentence.

70 of the Open school group (n = 100) had reoffended. Of these, 52 were in the penal system, 13 had been fined, 3 had suspended sentences and 2 had done community service.

The level of reconviction in both groups was not significantly different; nor did it differ significantly from the results found in the English system. Boys from the ex-Open school group showed a higher level of employment after release than did the Wing boys, and employment for ex-Wing boys was significantly lower than in the ex-Open school group.

Boys released from the Wing below school leaving age, 12 in number, all failed to attend normal school and were reconvicted. No boys below school leaving age were in the Open school group. A pilot scheme for aftercare involving local child guidance services was described.

The time scale for reoffending was highest for ex-Wing boys in the first weeks after release. For the ex-Open school boys it was lower (see Figure 8.2).

Mentally handicapped boys are found in both groups and these are discovered in the follow-up in the penal system.

Of the 12 per cent of the cohort who do not reoffend after release, there is a significant difference (0.05) in favour of those with intact families.

However, for the reoffending boys there is no significant difference whether or not the families are intact. In a group of highly selected boys by reason of previous convictions the family situation does not appear to be significant.

Offences are analysed and compared between the groups, and also between offences before entry into Forest and after release.

Ex-Open school boys collect significantly more charges for assault and breach of peace than ex-Wing boys. However, the only 'serious' charges are two cases in the Wing group.

Theft has decreased significantly and to one third of the pre-Forest level in both groups. Social security benefit and employment is now obtainable.

Car theft without other charges is not significantly different and is rare.

Care theft with other charges is identical in level in both groups but the level of such offences in ex-Wing boys is significantly lower than the pre-Wing figure.

Other offences appear, not noted before Forest, while some pre-Forest offences have disappeared.

'Untraced' boys were discussed.

The reoffending of the ex-Wing boys appears to be of a milder nature than that of the ex-Open school boys.

9 Summary and conclusions

This study has concerned itself with analysing two groups of boys, one in an open List D school and the other in a high security unit, 100 consecutive cases in each group, in an attempt to discern what differences determine the different placements. Are the groups truly different?

The relationship between genetics and behaviour has an uneasy history, having at various times been the subject of extravagant claims, bitter controversy and abiding ignorance. In the Forest boys it must have a part to play allied to social factors in that parents have died, separated, deserted, divorced, been murdered, been in prison or, for the illegitimate, perhaps unknown. Only half the Open school boys have parents still living together, and almost the same number among the boys from the Wing.

Of the intact families 12 from 50 fathers in the Open school are handicapped and non-wage earning; and 23 from 55 are in a like situation in the Wing. Mothers with handicapped husbands are not wage earning; but the mothers, where fathers are physically fit, are nearly all wage earning—and this in families whose average size is five children with a range from 1 to 14 children. In short, 62 per cent of the Open school boys have broken families or handicapped fathers, and 68 per cent are so situated in the Wing group, a difference which is not statistically significant. Thus about two thirds of the boys in both the groups have fathers (natural) who do not contribute to their support financially.

The families come predominantly from economically depressed urban areas and from districts where the teenage culture is delinquent and where social amenities are few or none. Fathers are mainly skilled manual workers (Social Class III) while the occupations of the mothers are more widely spread. Unemployment is low in the fathers, save for the handicapped. No boys from the wealthy, highly educated classes appear.

Apart from the greater number of handicapped fathers in the Wing group and the greater number of consequently housebound mothers, through a long category of comparisons, there are no significant differences between the families or family situations in either group.

Boys in the Wing group are significantly different from those in the Open school group only in that they have had many more placements in children's homes, hospitals, foster homes, assessment centres, List D schools, Longriggend or even prisons. They have also been significantly longer in the child care system.

In terms of intelligence both groups are in the normal range, a microcosm of any comprehensive school, with average, poor and clever children, normally distributed. This finding differs from the generally accepted view that delinquent boys are below average in intelligence.

Academic achievement in both groups is lower than the boys' potential probably due to low school attendance and despite education in List D schools.

Both groups, prior to entry to Forest, have a similar number of boys involved in theft (around 90 per cent) and in car theft (around 30 per cent). Other offences are low in number and do not differ between the groups. There are no serious crimes such as murder, manslaughter or rape. There are one or two boys in both groups who have no offences save school refusal or absconding. In each group also some mentally handicapped boys appear—around 10 per cent of the total cohort.

In the follow-up of boys after release information is derived from school records, a questionnaire sent to the boys' social workers, or from the records of the Scottish Borstal assessment centre. Of 100 released boys, 77 ex-Wing boys are known to have been reconvicted with 70 boys in custody. Of the 70 ex-Open school boys, 70 were reconvicted, with 52 boys in custody.

The nature of offences had changed since entry into Forest. Theft had decreased by two thirds, from 90 per cent to around 30 per cent. Ex-Wing boys had significantly fewer car thefts than previously, while the ex-Open school boys had an unchanged level. The ex-Open school boys had an increased level of assault and breach of the peace charges, significantly higher than that of the ex-Wing boys. The only two serious charges in the total cohort were for Wing boys, one having assaulted a policeman by stabbing while resisting arrest, the other being convicted of rape. These two crimes are not statistically significant in terms of the total group although grave in themselves.

The question therefore arises as to the efficacy of compulsory residential placement, in open schools or in a high security unit. Almost three quarters of the boys in both groups are reconvicted; the rest, in almost equal numbers, have disappeared from contact or have no known offences.

The ex-Wing boys, returning to society from a small, caring unit appear milder than the boys from the large open school. They disappear, however, more quickly into further compulsory residential placement, either into the penal system or back into the List D schools (for no boys in the study under school leaving age were able to return to normal school) and almost half are reconvicted within two months. The ex-Open school boys take around six months to reach the same numbers. Wing boys have a much lower level of employment after release, relating to the swiftness of reconviction, perhaps because 'labelling' prevents them from being employed.

Reconviction does not appear to be influenced significantly by the family situation, intact or non-intact, although the few non-offending boys, when both groups are counted together, do tend to belong to a nuclear family.

Prior to entry into Forest, significantly more boys in the Wing have been before the Courts for sentence than the boys in the Open school, who, in almost inverse ratio, have been dealt with by the Hearings system.

The study has examined in depth the two groups in a multiplicity of ways, sentencing, offences, families, previous placements, the geographical origin of the boys, the boys themselves and the ensuing history of the boys after release. Statistical analysis shows significant differences between the groups only in the aspects of sentencing, in truancy from school, the number of previous placements, the greater number of handicapped fathers in the intact families of the Wing group, allied to more housewife mothers, and in the swiftness of reconviction after release of the Wing boys, despite the relative mildness of their offences in relation to those of the Open school boys.

Clearly the groups are very similar in all other aspects. The reason for the incarceration of the boys in this study in the closed unit, the Wing, emerges: it is because the boys have persistently refused to stay in open institutions. It is not because they are more dangerous.

The sensitivity of statistical analysis is now being increasingly questioned as it gives only a broad outline of information, showing as it were a view from an aeroplane of a city. The present study allows only this overall sighting, showing the ground plan of the boys' lives and leaving much unknown and unexplored. To tell much more would burden further a study already overlong.

The melancholy deriving from the knowledge that so many boys go into further custody cannot be suppressed. Criticism does not centre around the care and concern given to the boys in the large open school and in the small locked Wing. All is done that can be done. Once released the boys are subject to the pressures and disasters that befell them before entry, and which in some cases find the boys more vulnerable.

Perhaps, indeed, society—in its present state of civilisation—requires these boys, just as the Athenians in the ancient myth required the yearly sacrifice of young men and maidens to the Minotaur. Embarked in a golden boat with silken sails and every luxury they sailed to Crete, expiating the guilt of Athens. Perhaps these boys are a similar sacrifice.

Bibliography

Argyle, M., *The Psychology of Interpersonal Behaviour,* Penguin, 1967.
Argyle, M., *Social Interaction,* Methuen, 1969.
Argyle, M., *Bodily Communication,* Methuen, 1975.

Bannister, S., *Scottish Borstals,* University of Edinburgh Studies, 1975.
Becker, H.S., *Outsiders: Studies in the Sociology of Deviance,* New York Free Press, 1963.
Becker, H.S., 'Whose side are we on?' *Social problems,* vol.XIV, 1967.
Belson, W.A., *Juvenile Theft: the Casual Factors,* Harper and Row, 1975.
Bowlby, J. and Fry, M., *Child Care and the Growth of Love,* Pelican, 1953.
Bowlby, J., *Attachment and Loss,* vol.I, Hogarth Press, 1959; vol.II, Hogarth Press, 1973.
Boyle, Jimmy, *A Sense of Freedom,* Canongate Publishers, 1977.
Branch-Johnston, W., *The English Prison Hulks,* London, Phillimore, 1970.
Burstall, Clare, 'The Matthew Effect in the Classroom' in *Educational Research,* vol.21, vol.1.
Burt, Cyril, *The Backward Child,* University of London Press, 1937.
Burt, Cyril, *The Young Delinquent,* University of London Press, 1944.

Cawson, P. and Martell, M., *Children Referred to Closed Units,* DHSS, S and R (Research Unit), 1978.
Cawson, P., *The Development of Closed Units and its Research Implications,* Research Division, DHSS, 1975.
Cawson, P., *Referrals to the Units and Behaviour Prior to Referral,* RD, DHSS, 1975.
Cawson, P., *Study of Staff in Residential Schools,* HMSO, 1978.
Charriere, H., *Papillon,* Panther Books, 1970.
Clarke, A.M. and Clarke, A.D.B., *Early Experience,* Open Books, 1976.
Clark, R.J.W., Personal communication, 1979.
Clarke, R.V.G. and Martin, D.N., 'A study of absconding and its implications for the residential treatment of delinquents', in *Abscondings from Approved Schools,* HMSO, 1971.
Clegg, A. and Megson, B., *Children in Stress,* Penguin Education, 1968.
Cloward, R. and Ohlin, L., *Delinquency and Opportunity: a Theory of Delinquent Gangs,* Chicago Free Press, 1960.
Cohen, A.K., *Delinquent Boys: The Culture of the Gang,* Chicago Free Press, 1971.

Cohen, A.K., *Deviance and Control,* Englewood Cliffs, Prentice-Hall, 1967.
Cohen, Stanley, (ed.) *Images of Deviance,* Penguin Books, 1971.
Coleman, J.C., *Relationships in Adolescence,* Routledge and Kegan Paul, 1974.
Coleman, J.C., 'Current contradictions in adolescent theory', *Journal of Youth and Adolescence,* 1978.
Cornish, D.B. and Clarke, R.V.G., *Residential Treatment and its Effects,* HMSO, 1975.
Criminal Procedure (Scotland) Act 1975, HMSO, Chap.21.
Curran, J.H., *The Children's Hearing System: A Review of Research,* Scottish Office Central Research Unit, HMSO, 1977.

Davie, R., Butler, N. and Goldstein, H., *From Birth to Seven,* Longman in association with National Children's Bureau, 1972.
Douglas, J.W.P., *The Home and the School,* McGibbon and Kee, 1964.
Dunlop, Anne, *The Approved School Experience,* HMSO, 1974.
Durkheim, Emile, *Suicide: A Study in Sociology,* London, Routledge and Kegan Paul, 1952.

Farrington, D.P. and West, D.J., 'The effects of public labelling, *British Journal of Criminology,* 17.2.1976.
Farrington, D.P., 'Truancy and delinquency, the home and the school', DCLP, BPS address, 1978.
Fiddes, D., *Personal Communication,* 1977.
Field, E., 'Thirteen year old Approved School Boys in 1962', *Home Office Research Study,* no.11, HMSO, 1971.
Finlayson, Alan, in Martin, F.M. and Marray, Kathleen (eds.) *Children's Hearings,* Scottish Academic Press, 1976.
Fyvel, T.R., *The Insecure Offenders,* Chatto and Windus, 1961.

Ginsburg, H., *The Myth of the Deprived Child,* Prentice-Hall, 1972.
Gittens, J., *Approved School Boys,* HMSO, 1952.
Glass, D.V. (ed.) *Report on Social Mobility,* Routledge and Kegan Paul, 1954.
Goffman, Erving, *Asylums,* Anchor Books, Doubleday & Co., 1961.

HMSO, *Children's Hearings.*
HMSO, *Children's Hearings,* Scottish Education Department, 1970.
HMSO, *Children's Hearings: Questions and Answers.*
HMSO, Children and Young Persons Act 1969, chap.54 (reprinted 1975).
HMSO, Criminal Procedure (Scotland) Act 1975.
HMSO, Social Work (Scotland) Act 1968, chap.49 (reprinted 1973).
Hoghughi, M. and Nethercott, S., *Troubled and Troublesome,* Aycliffe Studies of Problem Children, 1977.
Hoghughi, M., *What's in a Name?* Aycliffe Studies of Problem Children, 1969.

Imlach, A., Personal communication, 1979.
Jephcott, O., *Time of One's Own,* Oliver and Boyd, 1967.
Kahn, J. and Nursten, J., *Unwillingly to School,* Pergamon Press, 1968.
Klein, Melanie, *The Psychoanalysis of Children,* Hogarth Press, 1932.
Lambert, R. and Millham, S., *The Hothouse Society,* Weidenfeld and Nicholson, 1968.
Laycock, G.K., *Absconding from Borstal,* Home Office Research Unit, HMSO, 1977.
Leblanc, Marc, Address at the International Seminar on Criminology, Hamburg, 1979.
Lemert, E.M., *Human Deviance, Social Problems and Social Control,* New York, Prentice-Hall, 1972.
Lewis, D.O. and Balla, D.A., *Delinquency and Psychopathology,* Grune and Stratton, 1976.
MacIntosh, M., in Cohen, S. (ed.) *Images of Deviance,* Penguin, 1971.
McVicar, J., *McVicar by Himself,* Hutchinson, 1974.
Martin, F.M. and Murray, Kathleen (eds.) *Children's Hearings,* Academic Press, 1976.
Matza, David, *Delinquency and Drift,* John Wiley, 1964.
Mayo, P.E., *The Making of a Criminal,* Weidenfeld and Nicholson, 1969.
Mays, J.B., *Crime and the Social Structure,* Faber, 1967.
Mays, J.B., *Growing up in the City,* Liverpool University Press, 1954.
Meehan, Patrick, *Innocent Villain,* Pan Books, 1978.
Merrill, Eva, 'Glue sniffing' in *Community Care,* July 1978.
Merton, R.K., *Social Theory and Social Structure,* Free Press, NS, 1967.
Merton, R.K., 'The Matthew Effect in Science' in *The Sociology of Science,* University of Chicago Press, 1973.
Millham, S., Bullock, R., Hosie, K. and Frankenberg, R., 'Absconding' in *Community Schools Gazette,* vol.LXXI, no.7 and no.8, 1977.
Millham, S., Bullock, R. and Cherret, P., *After Grace—Teeth,* Human Context Books, 1975.
Millham, S., Bullock, R. and Hosie, K., *Locking up Children,* Saxon House Books, 1978.
Morris, A. and McIsaac, M., *Juvenile Justice?* Heinemann, 1978.
Morse, M., *The Unattached,* Pelican Books, 1965.
Nisbet, J.D. and Entwistle, J.J., *Educational Research and Methods,* University of London, 1970.
Nisbet, J.D. and Entwistle, J.J., 'Intelligence and family size', *British Journal of Educational Psychology,* 37, 1967.
The Pack Report, *Truancy and Indiscipline in Schools,* HMSO, Scottish Education Department, 1977.
Parsloe, Phyllida, *Juvenile Justice in Britain and the United States,* Routledge and Kegan Paul, 1978.
Petrie, Cairine, *Backward and Maladjusted Children in Secondary*

Schools, Ward Lock Educational, 1970.
Petrie, C. and Conochie, D.A.F., *Child Guidance,* Macmillan Educational, 1975.
Patrick, James, *A Glasgow Gang Observed,* Eyre Methuen, 1973.
Registrar General, Classification of Occupations. General Register Office, London, HMSO, 1960.
Reiss, Albert, Address at the International Seminar on Endangered Youth, 1979.
Rushforth, Monica, *Two systems of Committal to Residential Care: A Case Study in Juvenile Justice,* Social Research Branch, Central Research Unit, Scottish Office, 1978.
Rutter, Michael, *Maternal Deprivation Reassessed,* Penguin, Science of Behaviour, 1972.
Rutter, M., Graham, P., Chadwick, O. and Yule, W., 'Adolescent Turmoil: fact or fiction', *Journal of Child Psychology and Psychiatry,* vol.17, 1976.
Rutter, M., Tizard, J. and Whitmore, K., *Education, Health and Behaviour,* Longman, 1970.
Schur, E.M., *Labelling Deviant Behaviour,* Harper and Row, 1971.
Scottish Education Department and Social Work Services Group Residential Establishments (List D), November 1975.
Scottish Information Office Reference Unit, Factsheet, 1978.
Smith, H., Pharmchem. Research Foundation Newsletter, 1978.
Taylor, I., Walton, P. and Young, J., *The New Criminology,* Routledge and Kegan Paul, 1973.
Taylor, I., Walton, P. and Young, J., *Critical Criminology,* Routledge and Kegan Paul, 1975.
Trasler, Gordon, *The Explanation of Delinquency,* Routledge and Kegan Paul, 1962.
Trasler, Gordon, 'Delinquency', in Butcher, H.J. and Pont, H.B. (eds.) *Educational Research in Britain,* vol.II, University of London Press, 1970.
Tutt, Norman, *Care or Custody?* Darton, Longman and Todd, 1974.
Tutt, Norman, *Violence,* DHSS, HMSO, 1976.
Tutt, Norman, *Alternative Strategies for Coping with Crime,* Blackwell, 1978.
Vernon, P., Scottish Council of Educational Research in Education, Lecture, 14 September 1978.
Walter, J.A., *Sent Away,* Saxon House Books, 1978.
Walter, J.A. and Jones, Ray, *Community Care,* 9 August 1978.
Warnock Report, 'Special Educational Needs', HMSO, 1978.
Watson, J.M., 'Solvent Sniffing', *Nursing Mirror,* 28 October 1976.

Watson, J.M., *Lancet,* vol.XXXIII, no.4, July 1975.
West, D.J. and Farrington, D.P., *The Delinquent Way of Life,* Heinemann, 1977.
West, D.J. and Farrington, D.P., *Who Becomes Delinquent?* Heinemann, 1973.
West, D.J., *The Young Offender,* Duckworth, 1967.
Wiles, Paul, *The Sociology of Crime and Delinquency in Britain,* Martin Robertson, 2 vols, 1971 and 1976.

Index